GET MORE OUT OF YOUR MARCO POLO GUIDE

KU-603-037

1 go.marco-polo.com/lan

2 download and discover

GO!

WORKS OFFLINE!

<table>
SYMBOLS

INSIDER TIP	Insider Tip
★	Highlight
○●◑●	Best of...
⚏	Scenic view
⊘	Responsible travel: fair trade principles and the environment respected
</table>

**PRICE CATEGORIES
HOTELS**

Expensive	over 130 euros
Moderate	90–130 euros
Budget	under 90 euros

Prices for a double room, for
two persons per night with
breakfast (in a hotel); without
breakfast (in an apartment)

**PRICE CATEGORIES
RESTAURANTS**

Expensive	over 25 euros
Moderate	15–25 euros
Budget	under 15 euros

Prices for a meal with starter,
main course and a drink

LANZAROTE

ATLANTIC
OCEAN PORTUGAL
Azores (Port.) Cádiz

Madeira (Port.) MOROCCO

Canary Islands
(Spain) Lanzarote
Western
Sahara

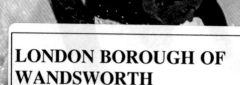

FREE!

THE
TOURING APP

shows you the way...

including routes and offline maps!

DID YOU KNOW?
Timeline → p. 14
Local specialities → p. 28
For bookworms → p. 50
Born in hell → p. 85
Movie set Lanzarote → p. 86
National holidays → p. 109
Budgeting → p. 113
Country living: Turismo Rural → p. 114
Currency converter → p. 116
Weather → p. 117

MAPS IN THE GUIDEBOOK
(124 A1) Page numbers and coordinates refer to the road atlas
(0) Site/address located off the map

Coordinates are also given for places that are not marked on the road atlas

(💭 A–B 2–3) refers to the removable pull-out map

INSIDE FRONT COVER:
The best Highlights

INSIDE BACK COVER:
Street maps of Arrecife and Puerto del Carmen

The best MARCO POLO Insider Tips

Our top 15 Insider Tips

INSIDER TIP **Heavenly drinks**
Star City serves up not just a stunning view, but also great cocktails. At night there's a sensational view from the highest building on the island, but it's just as good during the day when the eye is drawn to wave-battered reefs, beaches and half the entire island → **p. 37**

INSIDER TIP **Stately home with cistern**
Bucolically painted suites and romantic patios, underground white parlours and a chapel make the *Casona de Yaiza* a stylish sanctuary → **p. 87**

INSIDER TIP **Art to take along**
Green camel in front of a red volcano? Things have gone from down-to-earth to creative in this former village forge: the *Galería Yaiza* sells affordable art on paper, canvas and wood → **p. 87**

INSIDER TIP **Lovely souvenirs**
Attractive pottery and painted impressions of the island in the *Arte y Cerámica* atelier → **p. 30**

INSIDER TIP **At one with the Snow Virgin**
Climb to the chapel *Ermita de las Nieves* (photo above) for the most spectacular view of the island, plus sound effects from the pounding surf → **p. 56**

INSIDER TIP **In the house of Omar Sharif**
The charismatic actor lost this extraordinary property in a game of bridge. Luckily, you can now take a stroll through the labyrinth of halls and the passages in the rock at *Lagomar* → **p. 58**

INSIDER TIP **Like a mirage**
In the afternoon the *dromedaries* make their way back to the stables from the land of the pitch-black Timanfaya Mountains. A surreal sight, it could almost be a mirage → **p. 20**

INSIDER TIP **A taste of Lanzarote**
At the rural inn *La Bodega Santiago* in Yaiza, you can enjoy imaginative creations under the giant fig tree or in the quaint ambiance → **p. 87**

INSIDER TIP **Underground music**

Inside the lava caves *Cueva de los Verdes* and *Jameos del Agua,* you feel far removed from reality. Let this underworld impress you even more at a *concert* → **p. 108**

INSIDER TIP **Dine out with Orlando**

It's mainly locals who eat here. At *Lilium* in Arrecife, almost all of the ingredients are sourced on the island; the formula is fusion and the decor hip. And Señor Orlando serves Lanzarote's best wines → **p. 37**

INSIDER TIP **Wind down and relax**

It's not only the broad coastal landscape that makes *Lotus del Mar* such a fabulous place, but also the gleaming white houses flooded with light → **p. 47**

INSIDER TIP **Body & Soul**

Live out your creativity at workshops and then relax while enjoying professional treatments at the *Centro de Terapia Antroposófica* in Puerto del Carmen → **p. 66**

INSIDER TIP **Market madness**

At the weekend *mercadillos* specialising in crafts, farmhouse products and produce pop up everywhere. Probably the *Saturday market in Haría* has the liveliest atmosphere → **p. 57**

INSIDER TIP **Fish supper at sunset**

The fishing village of El Golfo (photo below) is always worth a detour, particularly at sunset, when the fire-red sun on the horizon sinks into the sea to the sound of screeching seagulls. The restaurant *Casa Rafa* boasts not just a menu of delicious seafood, but also a good house wine on the terrace → **p. 83**

INSIDER TIP **Fine dining in a cistern**

César Manrique turned *Los Aljibes de Tahiche,* two cisterns with thick lava walls, into a restaurant. Today it serves up hearty, charcoal-grilled meat dishes accompanied by homemade, unfiltered beer → **p. 46**

BEST OF...

● *Give aloe vera a try*

You can see how this desert plant grows at *Lanzaloe,* a small planta-
tion on the northern tip of the island. Precision cuts are used to ex-
tract the mineral-rich gel that is used in cosmetics and food. Taste the
aloe cake and liqueur without having to make a purchase → p. 48

● *For the sure-footed*

There is normally an admission charge to see César Manrique's landscape artworks, such as the Mirador del Río, the viewing platform
over the straits between Lanzarote and the neighbouring island of La
Graciosa. Just as spectacular, but free, is the view from the *Mirador
de Guinate*, and, what's more, it's quite likely that you will have the
place to yourself → p. 58

● *A lesson in vulcanology*

The *Visitor Centre* at Timanfaya National Park impresses with a fascinating multi-media introduction to the geology of the world's volcanoes → p. 75

● *Sunbathe in comfort*

The beaches in *Puerto del Carmen* are very pretty and very popular. If
you'd like to bask in the sun in greater comfort, then you have to pay
for a lounger. But after 5pm all the beach furniture is free – and there
will still be another two hours of sun to enjoy → p. 65

● *A walk with a view*

You can save yourself the car-parking charge for the nature
conservation area if you walk from the seaside promenade at Playa Blanca to the *Papagayo beaches* (photo).
And there's an added bonus: magnificent views over
to Fuerteventura → p. 85

● *To the heart of darkness*

Employees of *Timanfaya National Park* take visitors
where others can't go. The tour on foot explores
craters, tunnels and an almost level, solid sea of
lava in the middle of the Fire Mountains → p. 74

○○○● Dots in guidebook refer to "Best of..." tips

Wine from a volcano

The malvasia grape has an unobtrusive-aromatic flavour. Vines grow in lava pits, where moisture from the night-time dew collects. The accumulated water is then released to the vine roots during the day. Thus, even Lanzarote's stony wasteland becomes a fertile vineyard, and the wines from the bodega *El Chupadero* prove it (photo) → p. 68

Journey back in time

Nowhere else is Lanzarote's past more evident than in *Teguise*. In the *real villa*, the royal town, fine mansions and elegant town houses, narrow alleys, broad plazas and dignified churches gloriously reveal the island's history → p. 52

Salt from sun and sea

Nothing imparts a more intensive taste to our food than *sal del mar* or sea salt. This white gold is harvested in the *Salinas de Janubio,* where you can buy it cheaply at the *Bodega de Janubio.* Traditional dishes, seasoned with *flor de sal,* the delicately-flavoured "flower of salt", can be enjoyed nearby at *Mirador Las Salinas Casa Domingo* – an amazing place to watch the sun set over the shimmering pools of salt! → p. 85

Old sounds, new timples

The timple arrived on the island with the African slaves, its bright sound an essential part of the Lanzarotean folk song. This small stringed instrument is crafted by hand in small workshops, such as the one run by *Antonio Lemes Hernández.* In the attractive museum next door, you can listen to the sounds of this instrument and learn about others related to it → p. 55, 56

Beauty from the bowels of the earth

If you are taking a stroll on one of Lanzarote's lava-strewn beaches, be on the look-out, as you may come across a piece of *olivine*: a semi-precious, translucent olive-green gemstone, which looks at its best set in silver → p. 85

Forgotten recipes

There are still chefs around who love to prepare traditional dishes using ingredients sourced on the island. Two good exponents are the *Isla Bonita* in Costa Teguise and the *Casa Brígida* in Playa Blanca → p. 43, 79

ONLY ON

BEST OF...

AND IF IT RAINS?
Activities to brighten your day

● *Stark contrasts*

The sturdy *Castillo de San José*, high above the harbour at Arrecife, is the stunning venue for displays of modern art. The dark barrel vaults perfectly accentuate the brightly coloured, austere paintings → p. 35

● *Cave labyrinth*

Let your imagination run wild in the caverns of *Cueva de los Verdes*: think of what it was like to hide from pirates in this large cave labyrinth. To top off the experience, you'll also get a feel for the immense power unleashed by flowing lava → p. 45

● *Dive deep*

It's not just children who will enjoy the *Submarine Safari* (photo) and fascinating glimpses of marine life at a depth of 30 m/98 ft from a bright yellow vessel. Excursions start from e.g. Puerto Calero → p. 70

● *Lazy days over coffee and cakes*

The *Café La Unión* in Arrecife is a delightful spot to while away the days, if you cannot get to the beach. Follow that with a viewing of the artworks in the *Sala José Saramago* opposite → p. 36

● *An emotional roller-coaster*

You will need several hours to sample the many stations in the Roman-inspired bathing complex at the hotel *Costa Calero:* from a music pool to various saunas and the warm thalasso spa bath with massage. In the form of a wild river the pool flows out into the lava garden → p. 70

● *Eye to eye with a shark*

The 2 m/6.6 ft-long nurse shark Conan and a 1.50 m/4.9 ft stingray patrol the large tank at *Lanzarote Aquarium* in Costa Teguise – directly above the visitors. Or watch totally harmless sea cucumbers, clownfish and spider crabs → p. 106

RAIN

RELAX AND CHILL OUT
Take it easy and spoil yourself

● *Where the Canary Islands end*
From the *Playa de las Conchas*, the "shell beach" at the north end of La Graciosa, you gaze at wild waves and the scattering of rocky outcrops. Enjoy the quiet on Lanzarote's small neighbour → **p. 51**

● *The first bar in town*
When mariners arrive at the Marina Rubicón in Playa Blanca, they have to pass *Bar One,* outstanding in more ways than one. Nowhere else will you sense the yearning for the open sea more than here → **p. 79**

● *Water pipe smoking on a Bali lounger*
La Ola lies hidden away in Puerto del Carmen. Here you can relax on a four-poster bed, have a cocktail or smoke a hookah – all accompanied by the sounds of the sea → **p. 66**

● *Out at sea*
Out at sea, wind, waves and calm await. But if you are watching the underwater world pass by underneath a *glass bottom boat* heading towards Fuerteventura, it's even more meditative → **p. 107**

● *The perfect place to chill out*
Relaxed ambience all in white, palm fronds and a view out over the ocean, then add a cocktail and chillout music to dream by – the *Marea Lounge Club* in Playa Blanca is a place to unwind and be swept away → **p. 81**

● *Once a hermit's house*
For many years, a hermit known on the whole island lived in Yaiza. His estate *Casa de Hilario,* restored by an eccentric art-lover, is now an exclusive country hotel and the perfect refuge for those in search of tranquillity (photo) → **p. 87**

● *Sail away!*
As soon as the ferry leaves Órzola's harbour, your real holiday begins. Already on the way to *La Graciosa*, it will seem like you have left the entire world behind you, including the crowds of tourists! → **p. 49**

INTRODUCTION

DISCOVER LANZAROTE!

Look out the window as your plane descends; it is as if you are arriving on the set for a *science-fiction film*. Suddenly, emerging from a steel-blue sea, is this picture of bare, beige-grey hills, black fields of lava and craters, a *lunar landscape* of totally unreal colours and shapes, onto which scudding clouds cast their shadows, while the surging spray of the Atlantic Ocean showers over its shores.

At first sight, Lanzarote looks quite different to the other component parts of the *Canary Islands*, which, even in antiquity, were fêted as the "Blessed Islands" because of their benign climate. In some ways the fourth-largest of the seven Islas Canarias resembles a desert. It was in the Tertiary era, over 20 million years ago, when huge volumes of *basalt magma* broke through the fault lines in the earth's crust to form the two oldest islands in the archipelago, Fuerteventura and Lanzarote. Since then the Canaries have never been totally free of seismic activity. None of the other islands has seen such volcanic turbulence as Lanzarote. Until 1736 over 20 percent of the 307 square miles of the island's surface was reconfigured by *lava and ash*. But it is actually this seemingly bleak, barren and forbidding wasteland that makes Lanzarote unique. The *volcanic heart* of the island with its sparse, bright green vegetation is an

Photo: Papagayo Beach at the Punta del Papagayo

Summer, sun, a red convertible and the exotic valley of Haría – what more could you wish for?

unparalleled spectacle of the natural world, together with the equally unmistakeable feature of traditional villages with white façades and green windows and doors. The fact that so many settlements radiate in these striking classic colours is due to the work of Lanzarote's most famous son, *César Manrique*. No other island in the archipelago can boast as many pieces of (landscape) art by the great painter, sculptor and architect as this land of volcanic fire, which extends for just 60 km (37 miles) from its north-eastern tip to its south-western corner and only 20 km (12.5 miles) from east to west.

Before 800 BC
Homer and other poets of antiquity describe the Canary Islands as the "Islands of the Blessed"

1312
A Genoese navigator, Lancelotto Malocello, lands on Lanzarote and builds a fortress near Teguise. Lanzarote later takes its name from him

1402
The Norman Jean de Béthencourt conquers Lanzarote for the Castilian crown, and subdues the aboriginal population

1433–1479
The Portuguese and the Spanish quarrel over the Canary Islands. The islands are conceded to Spain under the Treaty of Alcáçovas

Of course you don't have to spend your holiday immersed in culture, even though it is spectacular on Lanzarote. The alternative is called *Vamos a la Playa!* Swimming, snorkelling, relaxing under palm trees – all year round! All three holiday resorts – Costa Teguise, Puerto del Carmen and Playa Blanca – have good *beaches with soft white sand*, in part protected by wave breakers. Or would you prefer something active? Not a problem! You can go diving, surfing or fly across the water on a jet ski. The island's well-developed water-sports infrastructure provides equipment and instruction. Less athletic tourists can watch Lanzarote's coastline glide by from a boat – a very nice way to spend the day! The island's year-round mild temperatures encourage tourists to outdoor activities off the water as well. Road bikers love Lanzarote because it is relatively *flat but diverse*. And the volcanic mountains draw a surprising number of hikers – the lack of vegetation does not seem to bother them. Golfers enjoy putting away on two courses, while hang gliders jump off the mountains to the north, landing softly in the *dunes of Playa de Famara*.

The *mild climate* is attributable to the north-east trade winds, which deliver rain to the other islands in the archipelago. Lanzarote's bad luck is that the highest peak, Peñas del Chache in the

Lunar landscapes, golden beaches and wines with a difference

1730–1736
Numerous volcanic eruptions devastate the south of Lanzarote. Many islanders emigrate to Latin America

1852
Arrecife becomes the island's capital

1936
General Franco, the military commander of the Canary Islands, stages a coup against the government in Madrid. The Spanish Civil War begins

1960 onwards
Tourism replaces agriculture as the island's main business

1975
Following Franco's death, democratic government is restored to Spain. Tourism takes off

northern Risco de Famara range, measures only 671 m(2200 ft) in height, too low to trigger proper rainfall from the clouds. The trade winds help to moderate the heat, as does the Canary Current, a coolish reverse flow in the Gulf Stream system. Little is known about the island's *original inhabitants*, known as the Majos. They probably came to Lanzarote from North Africa in the 5th century BC or later, and are genetically related to the light-skinned Berber peoples who still live there. They lived from fishing and growing cereals, which were ground in primitive mills into *gofio*, a type of flour and the *main staple in the diet of the early Canarians*. They also bred sheep and goats. Nowadays, however, it would be impossible for the lanzaroteños to live off farming and fishing alone.

Thus, most of the 142,000 inhabitants earn their living from the 1.5 million holiday-makers who come to the island every year. Many local people work as receptionists, cooks, porters, cleaners, gardeners or travel guides. The insecure nature of their livelihood stands in stark contrast to the everlasting beauty of the island: The work is mainly seasonal and with *unemployment at around 30 percent* of the population, all who

> **The whole of Lanzarote – a Biosphere Reserve**

have a job at all consider themselves to be very lucky. Most of the people employed in *tourism* live in the capital, Arrecife, and in the suburbs of Playa Honda and Tías, which have grown dramatically in recent years. The uniform and rather bleak high-rise blocks in the new districts contrast with the pretty villages in the hinterland, where the high-income earners have built luxurious properties.

The island itself has had to come to grips with all these changes, too. The wells ran dry a long time ago, so *desalination plants* now supply the island's drinking water. This is expensive to produce and also to supply. *Wind farms* reach up to the sky, strips of asphalt snake through the fields of lava. The lanzaroteños have for a long time successfully avoided the eyesores that tarnish the vistas in the tourist hotspots on Gran Canaria and Tenerife, thanks largely to the efforts of César Manrique. As a result of his work, in 1993 the island was awarded the coveted *Unesco Biosphere Reserve* status. Unesco were particularly impressed by the fact that almost 70 percent of the island's surface area – including a large national park – is a protected zone, and that the small

1986
Spain becomes a member of the European Community

1993
UNESCO awards Biosphere Reserve status to Lanzarote

2000 onwards
Despite a pause in construction work, more large hotels are built

2010–2015
The global financial and economic crisis hits Spain hard. The construction industry collapses; almost 30 percent of all Canarians are out of work. Oil drilling begins to take place (temporarily) before the coast of Lanzarote

2017
Europe's first underwater museum would like to improve Lanzarote's "green" image

On the promenade, the capital of Arrecife presents itself in its best light

offshore archipelago (Archipiélago Chinijo, which includes La Graciosa, Alegranza and Montaña Clara), had been designated as Spain's first marine reserve. Another positive feature was that a *traditional style of architecture in keeping with the landscape* predominated. However, Unesco is now considering whether to strip Lanzarote of its Biosphere Reserve status, because within only a few years, the small fishing village of Playa Blanca has become a *mega holiday resort*, and in Las Breñas and Puerto Calero holiday villages for prosperous Europeans have sprung up like mushrooms. In the meantime Spain's highest court has ruled that almost all the new hotels in Playa Blanca are illegal because their *construction permits were bought with bribes*. The mayor of Yaiza has also been sentenced for abuse of office. He supposedly pocketed 1.2 million euros for signing off on the permits for thousands of new hotel rooms.

> **Pause to let the peace and tranquillity work its magic on you**

Only in hidden corners, in villages well away from the main holiday centres, does one get the sense that Lanzarote, unlike all the other Canary Islands, is still a place of *privation, repose and tranquility*. This can often be seen in the faces of the older rural population: farmers with a *mule-drawn plough* stoically turning over the dusty soil, farmers' wives harvesting fruit from endless rows of prickly pears, old men gathered in the *village square* idly passing the time of day. The Lanzarote of yesteryear lives on only here, and only those who go in search of it with open eyes and receptive ears, pausing as they look and listen, will discover the island's true magic.

WHAT'S HOT

1 Microbreweries

Tap your own Many young Lanzaroteños who became unemployed during the crisis gave self-employment a try and began to brew their own beer. As did Alejandro, Rubén, Miguel and Elena, who make a naturally cloudy beer under the brand name Nao in the harbour district of Arrecife. You can try some, e.g. at the brewery pub *Cervecería Nao (C/ Foque 5 | Arrecife | naobeer.com)*. A number of microbreweries give Nao some competition, such as *Cervezas Malpeis (C/ Malagueña | www.cervezasmalpeis.com)* in Tinajo.

Animal-free

2

Vegan Lanzarote The trend came late to the island, but vegan restaurants are now popping up all over the place! Proprietors Susana and Fedra serve fresh vegetables at the *Pura Vida Arte y Café (Plaza de San Roque 3)* in Tinajo. A larger selection can be enjoyed at *Green Tara (C/ Mayor)* in the "town of the natives" Playa Honda – their veggie stews *(photo)* are known all over the island. Even in the capital diners are increasingly choosing the meatless option – at best at the lagoon: *El Veganito del Charco (C/ Jacinto Borges 11)*.

3 Artistic

Exclusively from Lanzarote Made in China is taboo, made in Lanzarote is all the rage: Barbara and Maurizio sell original decorative pieces made out of driftwood and recycled materials under the brand name Jardín del Mar *(www.jardindelmar.es)*. The motifs are inspired by the island, which is why many of the paintings feature Lanzarote's volcanic landscapes. Local artworks are on exhibit at galleries such as the *Galeria de Arte Enmala (winter Fri–Sun noon–6pm, summer 4pm–9pm | Mala | C/ Lomo de la Cruz 2B)*, which also has a terrace café.

Todo de la tierra

Organic from the island The trend for healthy, regional foods has also arrived on Lanzarote. Should it do some good at the same time? Not a problem! Cactus fruits, grapes and bananas *(photo)* are harvested by people with disabilities on an organic finca near Haría. The fruit is carefully dried by solar energy for two days, then bagged and sold in decorative packages under the label Grevislan *(www.adislan.com)* at stores such as the *Mercado Municipal de Abastos (Tue–Fri 9am–1pm | C/Longuera 4)* in Haría. The mercado also stocks other regional organic products such as herbs, sweet potatoes, onions, jams, cheese and yogurt.

A source of beauty

In harmony Lanzarote's black volcanic soil can bestow beauty, but is not the only ingredient used in local beauty treatments. Aloe vera and island vines leave the skin smooth to the touch while the sea salt from Lanzarote's coast cleanses the body. Black volcanic soil is used for massages and peelings *(photo)* at the *Centro de Terapia Antroposófica (C/ Salinas 12 | Puerto del Carmen | www.centro-lanzarote.de)* on the Finca Lomos Altos, while the many minerals, fruit and amino acids of the common ice plant, a plant native to the island that has perfectly adapted to the sunny and salty conditions, provide relief to those suffering from neurodermatitis. Seawater is the active ingredient used for thalassotherapy at the *Princesa Yaiza (Av. Papagayo 22 | Playa Blanca | www.princesayaiza.com),* while the vines and aloe vera native to Lanzarote make the skin radiant and soft at the spa *Hesperia Lanzarote (Urbanización Cortijo Viejo | Puerto Calero | www.hesperia-lanzarote.com) (photo).*

IN A NUTSHELL

TOURIST VEHICLES

It is a truly amazing sight: long caravans picking their way slowly across the ash mountains in the Timanfaya National Park. Lanzarote's dromedaries are among the island's main tourist attractions. These single-humped beasts of burden, also known as the Arabian camel, almost certainly arrived on the island with the first Europeans. They make perfect working animals, as they can, if necessary, go for weeks without water and will carry heavy loads over long distances without complaint. They were used in the fields, to carry goods and to operate gofio mills, and can also be ridden like a horse.

It was thought that the introduction of the combustion engine would end their career. But tourism has given the dromedaries a new lease of life. Now, every day, hundreds of holidaymakers climb into the saddle on the side of the hump and take a rocking ride through the Fire Mountains in Timanfaya. Dromedaries are bred near the village of Uga. Every afternoon INSIDER TIP between 3pm and 4pm the weary caravan heads home from the National Park – photo essential!

CONFLICT-ADVERSE RABBITS

The islanders categorically refuse to be lumped together with their brothers and sisters from the Spanish mainland. "We are Canarians," they will tell anyone who is willing to listen. "We speak, feel and act differently than they do!"

Photo: Dromedaries in the Montañas del Fuego in Timanfaya National Park

How do vines thrive with no rain? Are dromedaries fireproof? What are beetles doing in a cocktail? Lanzarote's secrets unravelled

The feeling is definitely mutual. Many on the Spanish mainland not only agree with this, they also ascribe a multitude of unflattering attributes to the inhabitants of the faraway Canary Islands: they are *aplatanados*, i.e. soft as bananas *(plátano* = banana), wishy-washy and adverse to conflict.

Canarians are truly a breed of their own: a blend of nationalities that has developed over many hundreds of years and includes Berber indigenous people and Spanish conquistadors, Portuguese set-

tlers and African slaves. Just as the archipelago as a whole sets great store by its distinctiveness, the inhabitants of each of the islands celebrate that which makes them special. And this certainly also includes nicknames: the Lanzaroteños, for example, call themselves Conejeros, which can be roughly translated as "those of the rabbit island".

The name goes back to a period when the new Spanish owners of the island released rabbits on the desert island for hunting. Wild rabbits may be just a distant memory now, but the nickname has stuck. And it is used with pride: no matter whether it is a bodega, restaurant or car rental company, "Los Conejeros" (pronounced: "Konecheros") is a popular addition to any company name.

A BEETLY COLOUR

Many people think it's some sort of bad joke, but it's true: The striking red colouring of Campari comes from beetle

The bugs cluster on the cactus leaves, feeding on the plants' sap. They then multiply rapidly. Every two to three months, the new larvae are removed manually from the prickly opuntia plants using a scraper. When they have been cleaned, they are killed by immersion in hot water, dried, ground and mixed with aluminium or calcium salts. Millions of the insects die to make a kilo of cochineal dye.

Initially, the future for cochineal breeding was rosy, but already a generation later,

Cochineal red: the vibrant red dye is made with crushed cochineal beetles

blood. If you are not convinced, you can check it out for yourself on Lanzarote. Growing on the many acres of land between Guatiza and Mala is an abundance of prickly (or cactus) pears. The plant's Latin name is opuntia and it is native to Mexico, but it is also the favourite food of the cochineal beetle. And this tiny, grey-white scale insect produces carminic acid, from which the crimson-coloured dye carmine is derived.

after the invention of cheap, synthetic aniline dyes, prospects for the business started to fade. Natural cochineal red is still used in some foods (sweets, liqueurs), cosmetics and medicines. Products made using cochineal, e.g. soaps, bath essences and peeling masks, may be purchased in Punta Mujeres at *Aloe Vera House (Mon–Sat 10am–6pm, Sun 10am–5pm | C/ Jameos del Agua 2 | www. aloepluslanzarote.com)*.

Since 2016, "Cochinilla de Canarias" is allowed to bear the EU label "protected designation of origin". This stresses its originality: the beetle species, its cactus host plant and the natural production process are unique in Europe.

PERFECTLY ADAPTED

At first sight Lanzarote might seem totally lifeless. But thousands of wild flowers, many of which only occur on the Canary Islands, can be found growing on the island. These include the spring-flowering, white *tajinaste* (bugloss), the scented, lavender-like *retama* and the sweet and bitter *tabaibas*, squat bushes with fat, sausage-like branches emerging from between the rocks. Hundreds of types of lichen have invaded the lava, breaking down the once-molten rock in a process that takes millennia. The *cardón* is the best-known of the many varieties of euphorbia. Their long, spiny columns tower skyward like candelabra. Canarian date palms, whose overhanging foliage and orange-coloured fruit give the valley around Haría a distinctive African feel, are plants that only thrive on the Canary Islands.

But the weirdest of them is all is the *drago*, the dragon tree, that on Lanzarote only grows in gardens. A member of the lily family, it died out practically everywhere over 20 million years ago except on the Macaronesian Islands, i.e. the Canaries, Madeira, the Azores and the Cape Verde Islands. For the early Canarians the dragon tree, with its scaly bark, bizarrely-shaped, thick branches with clusters of sabre-like leaves and a trail of cherry-sized fruit, was regarded as sacred because of its precious resin. Known as dragon's blood, this fluid turns dark red when exposed to the air. They used it from early times in the preparation of medicinal potions and ointments.

LUCHA CANARIA

Lucha canaria or *Canarian wrestling* has been a popular pursuit on the island since the days of the early Canarians. This is a sport that is only practised on the islands of the Canarian archipelago, and thrilling contests are still held today. A team consists of twelve wrestlers, but they only fight in pairs within a ring 12 m (40 ft) in diameter and covered with sawdust or sand.

Battle commences from a starting position, i.e. leaning forward facing the opponent with his or her trouser leg in the left hand. Each contest lasts a maximum of three minutes. The *luchadores*, as the wrestlers are known, grasp their opponent using a variety of holds, the object being to grapple the opponent down on the sand. But what is required is not just strength. Technique and speed are also decisive. There are no weight categories. Thus, it is possible for a 55 kg lightweight to be facing a colossus weighing twice as much. Women are also involved in the sport. If an opponent is floored twice in a maximum of three fights, then the victor wins a point and the defeated wrestler has to drop out. The team that still has wrestlers on the bench at the end wins the competition.

Should you wish to be a spectator at a Canarian wrestling match and experience the atmosphere in the audience, there are arenas *(terrero de lucha)* in Tinajo, Uga, Yaiza, Playa Blanca and Tahiche. The competitions are usually held at the weekend, but an up-to-date listing of events is available from the tourist information office or you can visit *www.federaciondeluchacanariade lanzarote.com*.

JACK OF ALL TRADES

Just what couldn't this Arrecife-born polymath do? Painter, sculptor, architect, designer, writer, green activist, César Manrique, born in 1919, was successful in many fields and is, by a long way, Lanzarote's most famous son.

After his first exhibitions of representational pictures, in 1945 he moved to Madrid, where he discovered abstract art and quickly made a name for himself. In 1965 he left for the USA and stayed there for three years. But when the tourists started arriving on Lanzarote in 1968, he returned, so that he could be in a position to contribute artistically when the modern world arrived in his homeland. Manrique transformed tunnels of lava and caves into breathtakingly beautiful dreamscapes; he built monuments and wind chimes. He campaigned vigorously against a replication of the concrete monsters that had sprung up on the other Canary Islands. What he fought really hard for was the preservation of the island's landscape by promoting its traditional architecture. Facing considerable resistance, he persuaded the authorities to impose strict conditions on new construction work; he designed low-rise holiday villages himself and oversaw the conversion of hotels.

Manrique died in a car accident on 25 November 1992 near his home at Tahiche. But the foundation which bears his name, the 🌐 *Fundación César Manrique (www.fcmanrique.org)*, ensures that his "critical voice" continues to be heard. The exhibitions and workshops staged there address a wide range of topics, from art and architecture to globalisation, immigration, environmental protection and nature conservation. The foundation has set up museums in Manrique's former residences, which are worth visiting just to appreciate the architecture. His house in Tahiche (see p. 46), which is built within volcanic bubbles, is particularly interesting.

ONE HUNDRED PER CENT CLEAN

Better late than never: nature conservation is very much alive on the Canary Islands. The small island of La Graciosa off the northern coast of Lanzarote has sun, wind and (sea)water in abundance, which makes it the perfect place to implement a project to meet all power and water needs with renewable sources. Co-funded by the EU, the *Microred La Graciosa* project is working to take the 500 islanders off the grid *(www.lagraciosa digitalocho.blogspot.com)*.

FIREWATER

It is difficult to imagine a traditional household without a *pila*. The *pila* provides cool, fresh water without electricity or a refrigerator, and that even when the temperatures soar. The *pila* can usually be found in a shady corner of the courtyard enclosed in a wooden cage that is as tall as a person. When you open the door, you will see a suspended volcanic rock with fernlike plants growing on its outside. The stone is hollow so that water can collect inside it. The water slowly seeps through the porous basalt, in the process purifying and enriching it with minerals. However, the water is not only supposed to be pure, but also cold! Once it has been filtered, the water drips into a large-bellied clay jug that is saturated with moisture. This acts as a thermal barrier to its surroundings and keeps the water wonderfully fresh. It is the custom to offer each guest a clay cup of this delicious water. Even if you are not invited to a house that keeps this tradition, you can take a look at these small, but highly effective water cooling systems at the museum *Palacio de Spínola* in Teguise.

THIRST QUENCHER

Volcanoes, ash and sand plains are everywhere, whereas there's neither much rain nor ground water. But who, then, quenches the thirst of the hotel gardens, the golf courses and vineyards, manager of the Bodega Mozaga, had a bold idea. As part of his work as a marine engineer, he had been developing a system to remove salt from seawater so that ship crews would no longer be dependent upon fresh water. Now he asked him-

What hides behind this wall of graffiti? César Manrique's Volcano House in Tahiche

of the 14,000 inhabitants and 1.5 million visitors? Water is the most precious and most scarce commodity on Lanzarote. In the past, the islanders took their drinking water from wells, fed from the Famara Mountains along a system of long tunnels *(galerías)* to the settlements where it was needed, or else they collected rainwater in tanks, known as *aljibes*. The largest of these underground reservoirs, the *gran mareta*, was in Teguise.

Everything changed in the early 1960s, a time when dromedaries were still pulling the ploughs on Lanzarote's fields and farmers were bringing in miniature harvests. One day, Manuel Díaz Rijo, self: wasn't the island itself pretty much a ship lying at anchor in the Atlantic? And so he designed the first seawater desalination plant for Lanzarote – it was dedicated in 1965. From that day on, periods of drought ceased to be life-threatening. Today's seawater desalination plants use osmosis, a method by which salt is removed from the ocean by means of a purely mechanical procedure that conserves resources. Moreover, wastewater treatment plants have been built to recycle used water and all large hotels are required to have their own seawater desalination plants.

FOOD & DRINK

It is often said that Canarian cuisine lacks sophistication. But the islanders have honed their inventive skills over the years, in order to conjure up a delicious meal from very little.

The Lanzaroteans have had to overcome many hardships in their long history. No one could deny that. **Dry soil** and a scorching sun, and yet the people have always managed to put food on the plate. Canarian cuisine grew out of poverty.

Lanzarote's aboriginal inhabitants survived mainly on **gofio**, a flour produced from roasted grains of barley or maize. First the grains were crushed and then ground into flour in windmills. The beige-coloured or light-brown powder had a more or less unlimited shelf-life; it was versatile, rich in protein and also filling. The Majos always kept a sack of *gofio* in the kitchen and with it they created a wide range of nourishing dishes: it was **baked into bread**, stirred into soup and drinks, added to fish, meat or potatoes or mixed with honey and almonds as a dessert. Daily life without *gofio* was unimaginable. It is still produced and served up at the table, but nowadays the powder is made only from wheat or maize. In the era of pasta and burgers, *gofio* is no longer such an important staple.

On the other hand, **soups and stews** have retained their status as everyday fare. A *potaje*, that famous vegetable soup into which the cook stirred anything that grew, is still to be found on the menu in every restaurant that serves

Photo: Fried calamari

**Barren land, a scorching sun –
but you can still look forward to a varied
menu of countless culinary creations**

cocina casera or what we might call home cooking.

Puchero and *rancho canario* are heartier. Into these **thicker stews** goes the meat from chickens, cattle or pigs. Not to be forgotten is the *ropa vieja,* literally old laundry. The name quaintly, but clearly, refers to the origins of this country delicacy, i.e. the **week's leftovers**. Nothing was ever wasted. Influences from other parts of the world – the Canary Islands archipelago was once at the crossroads of international trade – are also still to

be found in the *cocina canaria.* Yams from Africa, **sweet potatoes** from South America and saffron from La Mancha appear in everyday dishes.

Meat and fish used to be served only on special occasions. Every goat was precious, as it supplied milk. The Canarian sun has always limited food storage times, and the Spanish settlers had to cope with this problem too. So any booty that arrived in the household was pickled in sea salt and turned into a spicy concoction known as *adobos,* marinades, in

arroz a la cubana – boiled white rice with fried banana, fried egg and tomato sauce; a simple meal with a Caribbean influence

bienmesabe – sticky, golden brown dessert made from honey, slivers of almond, egg yolk and lemon. Translates as "tastes good to me" and that is most people's reaction (photo right)

caldo de pescado – a watery fish soup with potatoes and herbs

carajacas – liver of veal, pork or chicken, chopped and marinated in a hot *adobo* (marinade or seasoning)

cherne al cilantro – pan-fried Canarian gilthead bream in a spicy coriander sauce

gambas al ajillo – prawns deep fried in olive oil with garlic, chillies and sometimes parsley (photo left)

gofio escaldado – *gofio* (roasted cereals) with a caldo de pescado stock thickened into a velvety, maize-yellow porridge, served with herbs and bell peppers

leche asada –the "fried milk", mixed with eggs, lemon peel, cinnamon and sugar, makes a milk pudding for dessert

mojo rojo – red *mojo:* smooth to runny hot dip made with red peppers, oil, garlic, vinegar and salt, and served with meat dishes and papas arrugadas

mojo verde – green *mojo:* same method as *mojo rojo,* but with green peppers and lots of coriander leaves, to accompany fish dishes and papas arrugadas

papas arrugadas – baby Canarian potatoes boiled in salted water, always eaten with their wrinkled skins *(arrugado)*; delicious with *mojos* or grilled fish

pella – loaf made from *gofio,* water and salt. Cut into slices and eaten with *sancocho canario*

rancho canario – hearty stew made from chick peas, potatoes, pork, pasta, onions, saffron, garlic, pepper sausage; sometimes served as a starter

sancocho canario – boiled, salted fish, usually eaten with vegetables and *mojo;* the traditional dish for Sundays

which fish and meat did not spoil. These *typically Canarian sauces* made from oil, vinegar, bay leaves, herbs and garlic are regarded as distinctive features in the island's cuisine.

Small but nippy fishing boats cast their nets into the waters off Lanzarote's coast and haul out *cherne, bocinegro* and *vieja.* All are species peculiar to the Canary Islands and many of them quickly make it into the island's kitchens. Tuna and sardines are always worth recommending. Usually they are served simply *a la plancha*, after sizzling in hot oil on a metal plate. The same is true of seafood. *Choco* (squid) and *pulpo* (octopus) are snacks eaten only with fresh white bread. And then there are *papas arrugadas* and *mojo*, Canarian specialities much loved by tourists. *Tapas* come from the Spanish mainland. These "lite bites" have now found their way into the simple bars and cafeterias, where lanzaroteños take breakfast and lunch. In the morning, it is usually enough just to order a *café solo* or a *cortado*, a small black aromatic coffee served with or without milk, plus a *bocadillo* (a large roll with a topping). At lunch time, i.e. from 1pm, it is the custom to sit at the bar by the tapas display cabinet and snack on a little bowl of *albóndigas* (meatballs in sauce), *boquerones* (anchovies), eaten deep-fried or *en vinagre*, or any other delicacies on offer.

In the evenings lanzaroteños devote time to their families. The evening meal eaten together with family does not usually begin until about 10pm. Suppers usually consist of light fare, which includes tapas, *salad and ahite bread*, occasionally fish or *potaje.*

Many families treat themselves at the weekend. After a day on the beach comes a meal in a restaurant, followed by the luxury of a dessert, perhaps even a bottle of wine. Lanzarote is – just after Tenerife – the largest wine producer in the Canarian archipelago. In recent years, many family-owned cellars have been modernised and *new bodeags* have opened. At the same time, the quality of the product has improved dramatically and the wines frequently win international prizes. Along

Well stocked and bottled: Bodega in La Geria

the La Geria wine route, many bodegas open for wine tastings and visitors are also invited to take tours through the cellars. By the way, lanzaroteños also love their beer. There are Canarian brands such as *Dorada* and *Tropical* as well as good *unfiltered beers* from Lanzarote. A large bottle of mineral water from Gran Canaria or Teneriffa is an essential accompaniment to every meal.

It's best to see out the evening in traditional style: with a bottle of earthy La Geria island wine and a *carajillo*, a strong and tasty espresso with a shot of brandy.

SHOPPING

The local markets are always a festival of colour, notably the Sunday market in Teguise. This little town is transformed into a bazaar of curiosities and kitsch, crafts and culinary delights. Usually the vendor is also the producer: an elderly señor selling hand-crafted cane baskets or an ageing hippie behind a table with lava jewellery. Arts and crafts have a long tradition on Lanzarote, but the skills only survive thanks to the tourist trade. The market in Teguise proved to be so successful that many more *mercadillos* or mini-markets have since appeared on the scene: in Costa Teguise on a Friday evening, in Arrecife, Haría and Playa Blanca on Saturday morning.

The local people are more likely to do their shopping in Playa Honda, a suburb of Arrecife. Here warehouse and outlet stores line the LZ-2 highway; not exactly sumptuous palaces of consumerism, but still very functional sales halls. You will find pretty well everything you are familiar with at home – with a little luck it will even be cheaper.

ART

Lanzarote is very lucky to have César Manrique, the best-known painter, sculptor and architect in the Canary Islands. Even twenty years after his death still inspires, the art world. An international community of artists has since established itself on the island. Their studios are to be found in a number of places including Arrecife, Yaiza and Teguise. For further information, ask at the tourist information offices. Teseguite is home to the splendid workshop and gallery INSIDERTIP *Arte y Cerámica (Mon–Fri 11am–5pm | Av. Acorán 43–45 | tel. 928 84 56 50 | www.aguttenberger.com | www.lanzarote-ceramic.eu)*.

EMBROIDERY

First and foremost comes eyelet and hemstitch embroidery, known as *calados*. If you pay a visit to the *Taller Municipal de Artesanía (Sat 10am–2:30pm)* in, you can watch how the delicate blankets, bedspreads, curtains and other textiles are created. One of Lanzarote's last basket-weavers also works there. The palm trees in the immediate vicinity supply the raw material for baskets, bags and straw hats.

FINE FOODS

Lanzarote's popular wine with its distinctive strong and fruity flavour is available

Lanzarote's crafts have adapted to suit visitors' tastes. But it's still fun rummaging around in the markets

in all supermarkets, but it's best to purchase directly from the bodega. Please note that the local wines are not suitable for storing. One unusual and original product is sea salt from the Salinas de Janubio. It is sold in small, decorative packs. Goat's cheese is just as much a delicacy as the hot and spicy *mojo* sauces. The latter are sold in preserving jars. The sweet dessert known as *bienmesabe* is sold in similar glass packaging. The above souvenirs may be bought in supermarkets, as can *ron con miel*. This honey rum is another Canarian speciality, but most of it comes from the neighbouring island of Gran Canaria.

POTTERY

Pottery is produced in the traditional way without a potter's wheel. The clay must first be worked into manageable lengths. The potter then lays them on top of each other, then they are rolled out and any unevenness smoothed with a sharp stone.

The natural umbra or russet colour in bowls and jugs has not been painted on. Tourists want colourful souvenirs, so many plates and bowls are now sold in fresh and bright colours. Clay fertility figurines in early Canarian style make very popular souvenirs, with many holidaymakers amused by their erotic details.

TIMPLES

Teguise is the centre of timple production. These small, five-stringed instruments that resemble guitars are also decorative masterpieces. Made by hand, they are usually adorned with elaborate inlay work. Timples still play an important part: No celebration, no performance of folk music, no singing or dance event can take place without these Canarian-style ukeleles. The timples seen on sale in markets and bazaars, on the other hand, are industrially produced. Lanzarotean *artesanía* is not inferior merchandise: The prices reflect the time, effort and skills of the makers.

ARRECIFE

CITY   WHERE TO START?

Seaside promenade: The best place to start a stroll through Lanzarote's capital is the seaside promenade. Park your car nearby (e.g. in the underground car park of the Arrecife Gran Hotel); the town is quite small, but the congestion can be frustrating. If you are arriving by bus, get out at the promenade, too. Walk along the beach as far as the information pavilion (Mon–Fri 10am–5pm, Sun 10am–1pm), which is close to the Castillo. Head inland along the León y Castillo pedestrianised street, which is close to the Charco de San Ginés, the town's lagoon.

MAP INSIDE THE BACK COVER
(129 C–D5) (*M* F10) **Arrecife is no beauty, but it does have a few quite attractive places such as the lagoon with its neighbouring marina and a beach that is protected by reefs. If you are curious to know more about life on one of the Canary Islands' capitals, then this is the place to come.**

As you drive in from the airport via the southern motorway, the changing character of the city becomes evident: First open and spacious, then narrow and confined, a paradox that is typical of Canarian town planning. The wide highway whisks you almost as far as the city centre; turn right and suddenly you are in a narrow alley. A little further on to the left and before you know it you will find your-

The island's capital has had a facelift. Its alleyways are an open-air stage on which the everyday life of the local people is enacted

self in the congested traffic chaos of the promenade beside the Playa del Reducto. Overlooking the Avenida Mancomunidad is the five-star Gran Hotel, a high-rise block that was left in ruins for twenty years after a fire. Considerable investment was required to restore it to its present grandeur. The former park, once the favourite haunt of the local drug-taking community, has undergone a full-scale refurbishment and is now a large open space with boardwalks leading down to the water.

The Islote de Fermina, a rocky outcrop stretching far into the sea, has also been upgraded. A number of attractive pools, the designs for which were inspired by César Manrique, have been created at its broad tip. Alas, the townspeople hardly had a chance to enjoy this area before it was closed when the economic crisis hit and fell into desolation.

Follow the coast road to the north, and after passing the Club Náutico you come to the Parque Municipal, an elongated plaza with trees, gardens

The thick walls of the Castillo de San José protect works by artists such as Picasso and Miró

and coloured paving, now a lively and attractive promenade. **INSIDER TIP** Calle León y Castillo starts on the other side of the road. This pedestrianised zone with its narrow alleyways takes you deep into the vibrant heart of urban Arrecife. Businessmen, mothers with children on one hand and shopping bags on the other, casually-dressed *señoritas* and Canarian *señores* with their typical wide-brimmed hats go about their day on these steets. Make sure to come early because the streets empty when it's siesta time shortly past 1pm.

Take a nice stroll across the drawbridge of Puente de Bolas to Castillo de San Gabriel. Then head back inland, where the church tower of Iglesia de San Ginés rises up between the houses. With its benches and shady laurel trees, the small plaza in front of the plain church is the perfect place to sit down and take a break.

Arrecife's jewel in the crown lies in the quarter behind the church and the market: the Charco de San Ginés, the small natural harbour. It is fun to walk once around the promenade lining its shores. At the eastern end is the fishing port Puerto Naos, where soon after sunrise large and colourful fishing boats arrive back in port with last night's catch. Nearby jetties will bring you over to the new marina with its stylish shops and restaurants, which has become Arrecife's pride and joy.

According to some, the marina is a masterpiece with its sleek yachts lining the long piers and bright, cubist-style architecture. Others, however, question who is supposed to populate this huge stretch of land wrested from the sea. A bit further away from the centre near the ferry docks, the small Castillo de San José sits up on a cliff. As in days past, it still marks Arrecife's city limits.

SIGHTSEEING

CASTILLO DE SAN GABRIEL ✂

This tiny thing with a few measly canons on its roof is supposed to be a fortification? The pirates certainly didn't seem overly impressed by it as they regularly dropped anchor at Lanzarote, looted villages and took hostages. The site chosen for the fort in 1590 is also rather odd: it perches on an island just off the coast that is connected to the city by means of a drawbridge. The dike continues just beyond the fort so that it is possible to walk quite a distance "on the water". A museum inside the fortress depicts the island's history from its original settlement to the Spanish conquest to the present-day tourism boom. Climb the narrow stone steps to the "upper deck" to enjoy the impressive view of Arrecife's coast. *Mon–Sat 10am–5pm | admission 3 euros*

CASTILLO DE SAN JOSÉ ★ ●

Almost 200 years had to go by before the Spanish king came to the realization that a second fort would be necessary. It was built above the fishing harbour along the coast road to Costa Teguise and looks remarkably like the first one. Inside, however, a completely different world unfolds: the *Museo Internacional de Arte Contemporáneo (MIAC),* the Museum of Contemporary Art (*daily 10am–8pm | admission 4 euros*). The names of the artists read like a Who's Who of Spanish modern art: Joan Miró, Antonio Tàpies and Pablo Picasso, to name but a few. One room is dedicated to Pancho Lasso (1904–73), one of Lanzarote's most celebrated sculptors of the 20th century. Thanks to César Manrique, the architecture of the Castillo shows a move towards the modern age: a stunning staircase built into a white tunnel leads down to the *restaurant* (see p. 36) on the lower level, where panoramic windows spanning the length of the room look out over the harbour. Make sure you also pay a visit to the ✂ viewing platform.

EL CHARCO DE SAN GINÉS ★

The harbour in the centre of Arrecife is a fine example of how to redevelop a run-down urban area. Bobbing up and down on the shallow water are brightly coloured fishing boats, which blend in with the striking blue and white houses. A promenade leads around the harbour. Restaurants set out tables along it when the weather is good. Snack on a tapa and relax while watching the fishing boats enter and exit by a canal.

★ **Castillo de San José**
The squat castle surprises with the admirable Museum of Contemporary Art and a stylish restaurant → p. 35

★ **El Charco de San Ginés**
This attractively renovated natural harbour is being transformed into a lively bar and restaurant quarter, surrounded by a pedestrian zone → p. 35

★ **Iglesia de San Ginés**
This plain basilica is situated beside an evocative, laurel-shaded plaza on the fringes of the Charco de San Ginés → p. 36

★ **Altamar**
A fabulous view of the coast is served alongside excellent food on the 17th floor of the Arrecife Gran Hotel → p. 36

MARCO POLO HIGHLIGHTS

IGLESIA DE SAN GINÉS ★

The three-naved white basilica blends in well with the small, tree-lined Plaza de las Palmas. In the cool interior, the beautiful wooden ceiling in mudéjar style, the black columns of lava stone and the stone circular arches supporting the roof beams create a warm atmosphere. *No fixed opening times*

MARINA LANZAROTE

The modern marina with trendy shops and casual dining options links the fishing harbour and the ferry docks. It can be reached from the coastal road via footbridges. Be sure to stop by the local tourist information centre. It also sells **INSIDER TIP** souvenirs inspired by César Manrique! *www.ccmarinalanzarote.com*

PARQUE MUNICIPAL

West of the town beach, the extended promenade opens out into a small park full of exotic plants. Children can let off steam here on a playground with a skating park. The buses from Playa Blanca, Puerto del Carmen and Costa Teguise stop on the northern side of the Parque. This small bus terminal *(intercambiador de guaguas)* is worth noting, as the footpath to the town centre, which starts here, is a much shorter route than the one from the central bus station.

FOOD & DRINK

ALTAMAR ★ ⚶

A dining room with a breathtaking view along the coast and out to sea from the 17th floor of the Arrecife Gran Hotel. The cuisine is sophisticated and international – with matching prices. *Daily 7pm–11pm | Parque Islas Canarias | tel. 928 80 00 00 | www.aghotelspa.com | Expensive*

BAR SAN FRANCISCO

It has not really kept up with the times but is still a hotspot: The brightly tiled restaurant bar is always busy, from the first *café cortado* in the morning until the last glass of wine in the evening. Wide selection of tapas. *Closed Sun | C/ León y Castillo 10–12 | tel. 928 81 33 83 | Budget*

BODEGÓN LOS CONEJEROS

Reached via a narrow alleyway, this rustic-style restaurant serves authentic Lanzarote cuisine to a discerning clientele. *Mon–Sat from 8pm | Av. Dr. Rafael González 9 | Moderate*

CAFÉ LA UNIÓN ●

Of all the cafés on Plaza de la Constitución, this is the most welcoming. With its marble bistro tables and chairs à la Thonet, chandeliers and paintings, it has all the charm of a classic coffee house. Opposite in no. 16 stands the small, inconspicuous **INSIDER TIP** *Sala José Saramago*, a "branch" of the Fundación César Manrique. Art exhibitions are staged here at irregular intervals. It is named after the Nobel Laureate for Literature and Lanzaroteño by choice, who died in 2010. *Closed Sun | Plaza de la Constitución 16*

CASTILLO DE SAN JOSÉ ⚶

Dine out in a castle! The entrance of black lava steps and subtly illuminated walls looks inviting. Panoramic windows reveal a great view over the harbour, liveried waiters suggest luxury and sophistication. If you don't want to eat, just savour the atmosphere at the bar. *Daily | tel. 928 81 23 21 | Budget–Expensive*

LA TABERNITA DEL CHARCO

Not only the location on Arrecife's lagoon, but also the imaginative tapas and dishes created by Adela and Javier are definitely something to write home about. Try the sweet potato chips and the tender tuna, but make sure to leave room for a chocolate volcano dessert! *Closed Sun | Av. César Manrique (Charco) 52 | mobile phone 6 46 40 45 93 | Budget–Moderate*

INSIDER TIP fine view over the island's capital. *Daily | Parque Islas Canarias | www.aghotelspa.com | Budget*

SHOPPING

The pedestrian-friendly Calle León y Castillo and its side streets form the main

Not a bad idea: first go shopping for a bag and then fill it with the rest of your purchases!

INSIDER TIP LILIUM

Great cuisine at the new marina: Señor Orlando serves creative island dishes and quality wines by the glass. On weekdays there is an inexpensive menu, but by prior arrangement diners may try out eating blindfold, so total concentration on the taste buds is required. *Closed Sun | Av. Olof Palme | marina | tel. 928 52 49 78 | www.restaurantelilium.com | Moderate*

STAR CITY

The pub/café on the 17th floor of the Arrecife Gran Hotel can boast not just a a superb selection of drinks, but also a

shopping area. Modern retailers like Zara and Encuentro share the sidewalks with traditional shops.

MARKET

On Saturday morning, market stalls in the narrow lanes around the church sell arts and crafts and food. A smaller market takes place (for the time being) on Wednesdays at the Charco des San Ginés. *Sat 9am–noon | Plaza de las Palmas*

EL MERCADILLO

Nicely antiquated: Small retail centre with shops around a covered patio – including

Nothing going on? Don't worry, the lounge chairs are sure to fill up after sunset

an 🟢 organic food shop *(herbolario)* and a friendly cafeteria. *C/ León y Castillo 16*

PESCADERÍA MUNICIPAL & LA RECOVA
For self-caterers: fresh foods are sold at the small fish market and adjacent walled-in market patio until noon. *Mon–Sat 8am–1pm | corner Calle Liebre/Av. Vargas*

BEACH

PLAYA DEL REDUCTO
Treat yourself to some downtime on Arrecife's prime beach! It has soft white sand and is shaded by palm trees. The waves break on offshore reefs, allowing for worry-free bathing.

ENTERTAINMENT

CENTRO DE INNOVACIÓN CULTURAL EL ALMACÉN
The cultural meeting point of the island: there is something going on almost every evening – concerts, cinema, theatre, performance or art exhibitions! *Closed Sun. | C/ José Betancort 33 | www.cult uraalanzarote.com*

DOBLÓN GRAN HOTEL
at the Gran Hotel Arrecife: DJs keep the party going until dawn at the "Dublone". *Daily 11pm–6am | Av. de Mancomunidad 1*

KOPAS
Start the evening with cocktails and Shisha pipes in the waterside lounge, then dance the night away to salsa and house. Theme parties are often held at weekends. The disco is only open to guests 25 and older! *Daily 11am–4am | Av. Olof Palme/Marina | www.facebook. com/kopaslanzarote*

MULTICINES ATLÁNTIDA
Four modern cinemas, often showing international films – sometimes dubbed in Spanish, sometimes with Spanish subtitles. *C/ León y Castillo 42 | www.cines lanzarote.com*

location near the Playa del Reducto. The 60 rooms are clean, the bathrooms functional. Communal kitchenette for making tea and coffee. *C/ Democracia 11 | tel. 928 811008 | www.hrcardona. com | Budget*

VILLA VIK

This villa used to belong to an art-lover and is located just outside the town, but still within easy walking distance via the seaside promenade. This boutique hotel is designed in a modern, practical style, further enhanced by natural stone and stylish furniture. Suites with jacuzzi, plus large garden pool that's heated in the winter. *14 rooms | C/ Hermanos Díaz Rijo 3 | Urbanización La Bufona | Playa del Cable | tel. 928 815256 | www.vikhotels. com | Expensive*

WHERE TO STAY

ARRECIFE GRAN HOTEL

More than 160 modern rooms and suites in a first-class hotel in the town centre. With its ☆ **INSIDER TIP** spectacular view from the higher floors, own pool and spa, it makes a stay in the island's capital a realistic alternative. *Parque Islas Canarias | tel. 928 80 00 00 | www.aghotelspa. com | Moderate–Expensive*

MIRAMAR

The name pretty much says it all: you can enjoy the *mira mare* (ocean view) both from the balconies of the charming rooms as well as from the breakfast terrace and beautiful lobby. And the hotel is directly in front of the Castillo de San Gabriel. *85 rooms | Av. Coll 2 | Tel 928 81 26 00 | www.hmiramar.com | Moderate*

RESIDENCIA CARDONA

More basic, adequately furnished town hotel at reasonable prices in a central

INFORMATION

Parque José Ramírez Cerdá (tel. 928 813174 | www.turismolanzarote. com/en/arrecife), with a branch at the marina.

LOW BUDGET

When lanzaroteños are looking for bargains, they drive to the outlet and shopping centres in Playa Honda, a suburb of Arrecife. *Hiperdino* sells inexpensive groceries while *Centro Comercial Deiland* is the place to go for fashion, sporting goods and accessories.

At the *Pensión San Ginés (37 rooms | C/ El Molino 9 | tel. 928 81 23 51)* near the Charco de San Ginés, a basic double room costs only 30 euros.

COSTA TEGUISE AND THE NORTH

Exploring the north from the holiday town of Costa Teguise, you will encounter the many sides of Lanzarote – from the desert to the valley of palms, from dusty plains to the dramatic Famara mountains. And several highlights in between – each one with a "Wow!" effect.
Driving inland from the Costa Teguise, you will first see brownish beige hills behind which whitewashed houses are visible. Beyond Teguise the terrain changes, becoming more colourful. Here around Los Valles with its pretty terraced fields, the agricultural region begins. It benefits from its position at the foot of the Famara mountain range, which extends to the northern tip of Lanzarote. Here the trade wind clouds trigger vital rainfall. The pano-

ramic road winds up through fields of vegetables to a height of 671 m (2200 ft), passing the 🌐 *Parque Eólico de Lanzarote.* The dozens of wind turbines here produce a third of the power needed for desalination plants in Arrecife. In the west sheer cliffs drop 600 m (1960 ft) to the sea, while in the east the 12-million-year-old mountains run gently down to the coast.
During volcanic eruptions in the 18th century, the inhabitants of the Timanfaya region fled over the windswept Risco de Famara to Haría. Today still, this basin with its scattered, broad-crowned Canary palms and terraced fields forms the island's green heart. But the Famaras are also of volcanic origin, and here, you will see the circular, 609 m (2000 ft) Monte

Caves and fields, lava rocks and craters, beaches and cliffs – nowhere else on the island is as colourful and varied

Corona with the island's most impressive crater. When there was a volcanic eruption in 3000 BC – long before the island was settled – the Jameos del Agua and the Cueva de los Verdes, two amazing cave systems that can be visited today, were created.

Alongside the coast road to Órzola is the Malpaís de la Corona, the "badlands" of the Corona volcano. The sombre lunar landscape of sharp-edged magma clumps is even now, some 5000 years after its formation, of no agricultural val-

ue. Light green moss is the only form of vegetation on the lava-strewn wasteland, while tough tabaiba bushes with finger-thick branches have thrust their roots deep into the cracks. Given the inhospitable terrain, it is all the more remarkable that there are so many beaches of fine golden sand on this part of the coast. It's hard to resist stopping and taking a dip. Finally you reach the fishing village of Órzola, renowned for its good fish restaurants. Ferries to the remote island of La Graciosa leave from here.

Costa Teguise: white houses, black mountains and waves for windsurfers

COSTA TEGUISE

(129 D–E4) (*🗺 G9*) **Anyone who is just looking to relax a little on the beach has come to the right place at Costa Teguise. A couple of lovely small beaches with a promenade, a few windsurfing and diving schools as well as nice restaurants.**

The developed plots of land that extend deep inland clearly show the sheer size of the original expansion plans. But since the economic crisis, calm has returned and the authorities in Teguise are now inevitably pursuing a more leisurely development plan. As a result the holiday experience in the tourist village north of the island's capital is gentler than in lively Puerto del Carmen. Despite that some hotels here are reckoned to be the best in the Canaries, the five-star Gran Meliá Salinas being a fine example.

Not only the exclusive hotel, but also two other projects bear the unmistakeable signature of César Manrique: the *Pueblo Marinero* – the "mariners' village" – a pretty complex of several blocks around inner courtyards that replaces the historic town centre, and the *Villa La Mareta*, which can only be viewed from a distance. The magnificent estate was built by King Hussein of Jordan, who later presented it as a gift to the Spanish king, Juan Carlos I. Now this closely guarded mareta is used solely as a hideaway for the royal family, the president and foreign guests.

FOOD & DRINK

The trade winds that blow along Costa Teguise's coastal strip have always been a source of irritation for restaurant waiters. Much of their time was spent chasing flying table cloths. To prevent this many restaurant terraces today are protected from the wind or glazed with panoramic screens, so that waiting staff can get on with their work– and diners don't have to keep removing sand from their food and teeth.

BROWN DELI ☺

From breakfast to afternoon tea, this eat-in deli also offers takeaway menus. Opposite Pueblo Marinero, Tracy and Derek offer fresh food made with organic produce and local wines as well as superb coffee and home-made cakes. *Daily 9am–4:30pm | Centro Comercial Calipso | Local 2 | tel. 9 28 59 19 83 | www.brown deli.com | Budget*

ISLA BONITA ● ☺

Señor Pepe only buys from local farmers, as he knows that fresh ingredients taste best. Specialities include mild onions grown in lava trenches, sweet tomatoes and water melons, origin-protected lentils *(lentejas de Lanzarote)*, goat's cheese at all stages of maturity, kid and suckling pig. Then there's the

fresh catch from Arrecife's fishing fleet. The recipes are traditional Lanzarote dishes, spiced up and seasoned to perfection. Almost all of the wine is from the island. Give the organic wine from Bodega Bermejo a try. Also popular with the locals. *Closed Sun | Av. del Mar | tel. 928 59 15 26 | Moderate*

EL PESCADOR

Good, down-to-earth Canarian and international cuisine in the relaxing setting of Manrique's mariners' village. *Closed Sun and lunchtime | Plaza del Pueblo Marinero | tel. 928 59 08 74 | Moderate*

LA TABLA

An airy terrace (though not directly by the sea) awaits at this eatery. Sit back on your padded chair and enjoy the affordable tapas menu, with seven small dishes guaranteed to satisfy two people. If you are really hungry, then try

MARCO POLO HIGHLIGHTS

the charcoal-grilled meat dishes. The home-made desserts are also tasty. Friendly service. *Daily | Centro Comercial Las Maretas | near the post office | tel. 9 28 52 40 76 | Budget–Moderate*

VILLA TOLEDO

Restaurant with terrace right on the seafront above rocks – perfect at sunset. Large fish and meat menu. *Daily | Av. Los Cocederos | tel. 928 59 06 26 | Moderate*

SHOPPING

MERCADILLO

The Pueblo Marinero is the atmospheric backdrop to the Friday evening market (from 5pm): Artisans from all over the island sell lava jewellery and watercolours with Lanzarote motifs, fabrics and pottery.

LOW BUDGET

You can buy sandwiches and coffee for just a couple of euros at the *Bar Vali (daily 9.30am–1pm)* at the lower end of the Av. del Jablillo that leads down to the beach of Costa Teguise.

● If you want to admire the stunning view of La Graciosa at the ☼ *Mirador del Río* without paying the admission fee, get close to the cliff top some 200 m/656 ft left from the road.

Cool jazz music plays at *Chiringo Beach (daily from 11am | Playa de la Garita)* on the long beach in Arrieta where you can order inexpensive sandwiches and tapas. Come at the weekend for paella.

WINDSURFING CLUB

The venerable shop sells or rents out first-rate branded windsurfing equipment. Also windsurfing and SUP courses, snorkelling and kayak excursions. *C/ Marajo | Centro Comercial Las Maretas 2 | tel. 9 28 59 07 31 | www.lanzarotewindsurf. com*

ENTERTAINMENT

Only at the weekend do the clubs and bars in the Pueblo Marinero fill up. The nightlife is aimed primarily at British tourists. *Dicken's Bar (daily until 2:30am | Av. del Mar)* may sound Victorian, but it belongs to a Spaniard named Victor who mixes good cocktails and stocks a large selections of gins, including Canarian Macaronesian; live music several times a week.

WHERE TO STAY

BE LIVE GRAND TEGUISE PLAYA

The most impressive feature here is the extravagantly planted, multi-storey indoor plaza, ringed by galleries, from which 314 rooms can be reached. There's a circular bar right in the middle. This large hotel has several pools and also direct access to the Playa del Jablillo. *Av. del Jablillo | tel. 928 59 06 54 | www.beliv ehotels.com | Moderate–Expensive*

MELIÁ SALINAS

The amazing pool zone was designed by César Manrique in 1977; his idea of filling out the inner area with luxuriant gardens pointed the way for holiday hotels all over the world. Today, the five-star hotel has undergone a facelift. Several exclusive garden villas were added. *310 rooms | Av. Islas Canarias | tel. 928 59 00 40 | www.melia.com | Expensive*

INFORMATION

Av. Islas Canarias/Pueblo Marinero (tel. 928 59 25 42 | www.turismoteguise.com)

WHERE TO GO

ARRIETA (125 E5) (*CD H6*)

No wonder that Arrieta's star is on the rise: white houses line the oceanfront, a mole juts out into the water. Every day, fishing boats head out onto the ocean from here to supply the restaurants along the main road with fresh seafood. There is also a beautiful beach: the 800-m (2625 ft) long *Playa de la Garita* may be strewn with rocks, but in between glistens light-coloured sand. For sightseers the only place of interest in the town is the *Casa Juanita*, known as the Blue House or *Casa Azul.* An impressive structure, it was built on a cliff by a lanzaroteño who had amassed a fortune in Venezuela. The deep blue upper façade panelling shines from afar. Although it is not a museum in the strict sense of the word, the *Museo de Aloe (closed Sun | C/ El Cortijo 2)* on the edge of town displays all kinds of information about this "miracle plant" on the way to the actual shop.

Most visitors come to Arrieta for the fish restaurants. Situated on the mole, equipped with a large ship's telescope and offering a view of the Blue House is *El Charcón (closed Wed | tel. 928 84 8110 | www.elcharcon-lanzarote.com | Moderate)*, where Ricardo and Sabina happily dispense the INSIDER TIP La Grieta house wine. Their white wine, and the rather rare, for Lanzarote, red have designation of origin status. Always popular is a visit to *Amanecer (closed Thu | La Garita 46 | tel. 928 83 54 84 | Moderate)*, where a team of brothers cook freshly caught

fish without frills, but very well. The tables on the small terrace right by the sea fill up quickly.

Magnetic house in blue and red: let's go to the Casa Azul!

CUEVA DE LOS VERDES ★ ●
(125 F5) (*CD H6*)

TThe perfect journey into the underworld: descend into the bowels of a volcano! As your guide takes you down, you feel as though you are in a giant walk-through sculpture complete with ingenious lighting effects and spherical sounds. The Cueva de los Verdes is part of a 7.5 km (4.5 miles) lava tunnel, the *Túnel de la Atlántida.* The cave was formed when Monte Corona erupted 5000 years ago. Streams of lava, which at the time flowed into the sea, quickly cooled down at the surface, while the hot magma beneath continued on its

Don't get pricked: make sure to stay on the path at the Jardín de Cactus

course. When the eruptions stopped, the residues flowed out, leaving behind galleries and caverns at various levels, which together reach a height of 40 m/131 ft and extend far out into the sea. At the time of the pirate attacks the Cueva de los Verdes served as a refuge, as it was well hidden. In 1618, however, Algerian buccaneers discovered the caves through an act of betrayal and carried off hundreds of people into slavery.

The guided tour through this bizarre underworld inside the lava lasts 45 minutes and covers a distance of 2 km (over a mile). Halfway along there's a large auditorium where everyone can take a rest. At the end, there's another special effect, but we won't spoil the experience by giving away details. Concerts are held in the auditorium – a special experience! *Daily 10am–5pm | admission 9 euros (including guided tour) | www.centrosturisticos. com*

FUNDACIÓN CÉSAR MANRIQUE ★
(129 D4) (*∅ F9*)

Visitors to Lanzarote keen on gaining a better understanding of the island's greatest artist will almost certainly want to pay a visit to the Fundación César Manrique in *Tahiche*. The foundation occupies the artist's former home, which is situated near a roundabout showcasing a large Manrique mobile made from stainless steel. A large part of César Manrique's oeuvre and also pieces by his artist friends are exhibited here, but the extraordinary house alone is worth a visit: One remarkable feature is the section of the futuristic underground lounge built into lava bubbles. *Daily 10am–6pm | admission 8 euros | www.fcmanrique.org* Another remarkable architectural structure originally designed by Manrique is the nearby restaurant INSIDER TIP *Los Aljibes de Tahiche (Fri–Wed 11am–10pm | exit the roundabout towards Cos-*

ta Teguise | mobile phone 6 10 45 42 94 | *Moderate–Expensive*), built within a former cistern. A Brazilian-Argentine duo cooks up meat on the grill as well as good baked dishes that you can enjoy on the terrace shaded by palms and dragon trees. Make sure to check out the art gallery in the cistern!

GUATIZA (129 E2) (*Ø G–H7*)

Fields of cacti as far as the eye can see. Every open space in and around Guatiza is planted with the fleshy opuntia cactus. Farmers with low-fitting straw hats pass along the rows. An avenue of old eucalyptus trees runs through the village, which was once prosperous courtesy of the cochineal beetle. Although the trade in natural dyes is now over, between Guatiza and Mala the tiny creatures are still painstakingly harvested.

At the entrance to the village, the road branches off to the right to Los Cocoteros and one of Lanzarote's last functioning salt ponds. The *Salina Los Cocoteros* is easy to spot as it still uses wind-powered pumps. Seawater is left to evaporate in hundreds of ponds, and as the water disappears, it leaves behind a thick layer of fine salt grains.

The ★ *Jardín de Cactus (daily 10am–5:45pm | admission 5.50 euros)* at the end of the village is devoted to the spiny world of cacti. César Manrique collected almost 1500 different types of cactus in the broad pit of a former quarry at the foot of a restored gofio mill. The cactus garden was his final task. Fragments of black lava and high stone columns add to this bizarre setting, so it is not surprising visitors imagine themselves lost in an alien world. A restaurant here serves snacks and a shop sells souvenirs.

If you want to spend the night nestled between cacti and the wild coast, book one of the comfortable apartments decorated in Manrique-style at ☼ INSIDER TIP *Lotus del Mar (C/ El Cangrejo 31 | tel. 9 28 52 95 89 | www.lotus-del-mar.com | Budget–Moderate).* The gleaming white exterior hides a lovingly furnished, well-designed interior further accented by the views of the sea as well as the mountains from the different terraces. Nowhere else on Lanzarote is more restful! It is also a good address for allergy sufferers.

JAMEOS DEL AGUA ★
(125 F5) (*Ø H6*)

Hollywood diva Rita Hayworth considered them to be the "Seventh Wonder of the World". Even though this may seem a bit exaggerated, the *Jameos del Agua* really are something quite special: First, visitors descend through a wide funnel, a collapsed lava ceiling, and pass a subterranean, terraced restaurant overgrown with lush plants. Still deeper, an enchanting saltwater lake shimmers, home to a species of white crab that you can't see anywhere else in the world. As the creatures survive in the dark, they have no sight. A sign warns: Do not throw coins into the water, as the crabs would be poisoned by the metal oxide.

You climb up to a second cave on the opposite side of the lake. The roof of the cave is open so wide that the sun can penetrate down into the cave unhindered. Which makes this the perfect spot for a spectacular white pool surrounded by palm trees. In the next lava tube there is an auditorium boasting superb acoustics. Concerts are sometimes staged here.

Like the Cueva de los Verdes, the Jameos del Agua is part of the Atlántida tunnel system. Until the late 1960s farmers deposited refuse through two gaping holes *(jameos)* in the lava blanket. We owe a debt of gratitude to César Manrique for clearing out and saving the *jameos*. He retained the structure of this natural phenomenon, but transformed it into a magical work of art. And this was commercially successful, so as as result the artist gained assignments for further attractions. *Daily 10am–6:30pm; Tue, Fri and Sat also 7pm–3am with 45-minute folklore show from 10:30pm, after that DJ sessions until 12:30am | admission 9 euros | www.centrosturisticos.com*

ÓRZOLA (125 E3) (*∅ H4*)

The small fishing port in the far north of the island is definitely worth a visit, if only to watch ferocious surf crashing against the rocks. There are a number of rustic-style fish restaurants here. The ocean's harvest is served fresh in the INSIDER TIP *Os Gallegos (daily from 10am | C/ La Quemadita 6 | tel. 9 28 84 25 02 | Moderate)*, a restaurant at a prime location: everything revolves around freshly caught fish. Toni swiftly brings out the dishes his wife Begonia has prepared: tender Galician-style (i.e. cut into slices) Pulpo, mussels, prawns and overflowing fish platters. But remember to leave some room for the delicious desserts! Also good: *Charco Viejo (closed Mon | C/ La Quemadita 8 | tel. 928 84 25 91 | Moderate)* and *Perla del Atlántico (closed Mon | C/ Peña San Dionisio 1 | tel. 928 84 25 89 | Moderate)*. But people don't just come to Órzola to eat. Almost every hour, little boats shuttle between the port and the island of La Graciosa.

There are a number of fine beaches nearby. The spectacular *Playa de la Cantería* beneath the towering Famara Mountains can be reached as part of a walk. South-west of Órzola, only a few metres from the LZ-1, there are more magnificent playas to explore, such as the sandy beaches at *Caletón*

Blanco. Note here the striking contrast between the black lava rocks and the almost snow-white sand. Because the water in the sheltered bays is shallow, the sea is several degrees warmer than elsewhere and suitable for young children.

If you take the LZ-204 heading to Yé for 2 km (1.2 miles), you will come to the aloe vera plantation ● 🕗 *Lanzaloe (Mon–Sat 11am–5pm | C/ La Quemadita 96 | www.lanzaloe.com)*. Chemicals are not used here either to grow or process the plants. Try the free samples of culinary delights as well as cosmetics made with aloe vera.

TABAYESCO (125 E6) (*∅ G6*)

Tabayesco nestles amid steeply climbing terraced fields dedicated to the cultivation of vegetables and by the mouth of the fertile 🌿 Valle de Temisa. Among the crops grown by the villagers in their gardens are avocados, almonds, oranges and, unusually for Lanzarote, bananas. A winding road leads up into the Famara Mountains.

YÉ (125 E4) (*∅ G5*)

The village of Yé clings to the mountainside at a height of around 400 m (1300 ft) beneath the impressive panorama of the eroded Monte Corona. When arriving from Arrieta, before you reach the village, you will see the road to the quaint winery 🕗 *Monte Corona,* where you can taste local wines as well as cactus liqueur. From the first pressing to bottling, everything is still done by hand and no synthetic additives are used. The *Volcán de la Corona* restaurant *(closed Mon | tel. 928 52 65 16 | Moderate)* near the junction at the village serves hearty meat dishes straight from the charcoal grill.

LA GRACIOSA

(125 C–E 1–3) (ᵘ G3–4) Anyone wishing to make the crossing from Órzola to the tiny island of ★ ● La Graciosa day-trippers. Practically every house has apartments to let, there is a well-stocked supermarket and even a disco. But in the end none of this has very much to do with mass tourism Lanzarote-style. The *Playa de Francesa*, the *Playa de la Cocina* and,

For all those who weren't yet sure: you have arrived on the island La Graciosa

needs good sea legs: During the first ten minutes of the journey the small boats are buffeted by the high waves of the untamed Atlantic Ocean.

But once into the El Río straits the waves usually subside and the waters become much calmer. And that tranquillity continues on land. This island is a thoroughly agreeable relic from the past. Before the advent of tourism to the Canaries, this was what life was like on the islands – or at least very similar. The main village of *Caleta del Sebo* consists of some plain houses and only a few streets laid out at right angles, none of them made up.

But time has not left everything unscathed. There are a few restaurants, which cater for the needs of the many

above all, the *Playa de las Conchas* in the north rank among the finest and most isolated beaches in the Canaries. So La Graciosa continues to be an island haven reserved for a few beach joggers, walkers, bird-watchers and lovers of peace and quiet – at least for the time being.

What is certain is that the other, even smaller islands in the Chinijo archipelago will remain unspoilt for a very long time to come. *Alegranza* and *Montaña Clara* are not just protected nature reserves, but also much too wild and too remote. You can, however, go on a boat trip *(www.lanzaroteactiveclub.com)* and at least see them from the coast.

Passenger ferries (no vehicle transport): *Líneas Marítimas Romero (daily from*

Órzola at 8:30am, 10am, 11am, noon, 1:30pm, 4pm, 5pm and 6pm, from La Graciosa at 8am, 10am, 11am, 12:30pm, 3pm, 4pm and 5pm, additional connections in the summer | return crossing 20 euros, with bus transfer from the hotels in the resorts 29 euros | tel. 9 02 40 16 66 | www.lineasromero.com)

FOOD & DRINK

The two pensiones mentioned below have basic, but good restaurants *(Budget)* on their ground floor. Also worth recommending is the *El Marinero (C/ García Escamez 11)* near the church, which is run by the ever-present Romero family – most of the ferries also belong to this clan. More stylish: *El Varadero (Moderate)* right by the ferry pier. A little further on into the village by the harbour basin is the *El Chiringuito bar (Budget)*. This is the meeting place for the locals, fishermen and anyone else wanting to relax with a drink.

WHERE TO STAY

This guesthouse in the centre of the village can offer eight basic rooms with bathroom for the night. *C/ Mar de Barlovento 6 | tel. 928 84 20 51 | Budget*

PENSIÓN GIRASOL PLAYA
After renovation the "sunflower" is much more comfortable than in the past. It has rooms and also apartments in the annex, most with a fine harbour view. *C/ García Escamez 1 | tel. 928 84 21 18 | www.graci osaonline.com | Budget*

FOR BOOKWORMS

Mararía – written already in 1973 but still *the* novel of the Canaries: Rafael Arozarena tells the mysterious story of a woman from the Lanzarotean mountain village of Femés who was very seductive but fell victim to a dangerous liaison. Decades later a stranger arrives in the village and hears the tragic story of beautiful Mararía

Lanzarote – Michel Houellebecq's short book about Lanzarote (with a volume of his photographs) examines themes around tourism and hedonism

Obra Espacial/Arte y Naturaleza – The Fundación César Manrique sells these two DVDs, which explore his contributions to the island's architecture and art

There's always another volcanic cone in the way: hikers on the Isla Graciosa

HIKES

There is a wide selection of hikes to choose from on La Graciosa. Hikers who consider themselves to be in good shape could climb either of the following volcanoes from its less steep side: the ☼ *Montaña del Mojón* in the middle of the island and the ☼ *Montaña Bermeja* in the north. But the island is too large to get round all in one day. Some walkers may prefer to join a guided tour, in which case they can call on the services of ● *Explora La Graciosa (C/ Popa 15 | Caleta del Sebo | tel. 928 84 21 94 | exploralagraciosa@gmx.net)*. Eva Maldener, who has lived on the island for more than a decade, offers walks focussing on La Graciosa's flora and history– choose a half-day or a whole day walk. She will also help out if you are looking for accommodation on the island.

The two varied circular walks described below may be undertaken independently. Neither is too strenuous.

INSIDER TIP NORTHERN ROUTE

A track leads through the middle of the island from Caleta del Sebo and between the two volcanic cones of the Montaña del Mojón and the Agujas Grandes and then through to the ● INSIDER TIP *Playa de las Conchas*. This beach must be one of the finest on the Canary Islands. But because of the strong waves and currents the waters here are dangerous even for experienced swimmers. Below the Montaña Bermeja turn towards the north coast to reach the spectacular dunes near *Playa Lambra*. You can't miss the astonishing sight of countless millions of shells, in places completely covering the surface of the sand. Return to the harbour at Caleta via the village of *Pedro Barba*, which is not permanently inhabited. *Approx. 16 km/10 miles or 4 hours*

SOUTHERN ROUTE

If you choose the southern route, leave Caleta along the harbour basin. When you reach the pretty *Playa del Salado*, look out for a track, which you should follow. If walking in the hot sun, it's worth going a little further south for two even more beautiful beaches, the *Playa Francesa* and the *Playa de la Cocina*. Now return a short distance and on the shore side pass below the *Montaña Amarilla*, the "yellow mountain", to reach the west coast. There you will join a track, which first passes vegetable fields and then, keeping the Montaña always on the right-hand side, returns to Caleta del Sebo. *Approx. 10 km/6 miles or 2.5 hours*

WHERE TO GO

ALEGRANZA (O) (📖 G1)

La Graciosa's smaller neighbouring island is not open to visitors, but you can get to know its spectacular coastline on a boat trip *(www.lanzaroteactiveclub.com)*. This inhospitable island of only 12 km² (4.5 square miles) a few miles north of La Graciosa, is no longer inhabited. Like the whole "small archipelago" *(Archipiélago Chinijo)*, it is now a nature conservation area. The marine life here is unspoilt and varied, and many rare bird species nest on the island, among them a big rookery of Scopoli's shearwater birds.

TEGUISE

(128–129 C–D2) (📖 F7–8) **When you arrive in ⭐ ● Teguise (pop. 17,000), it will seem as if you have made a journey back in time. You will be greeted by grand villas with high wooden portals and then have to squeeze through narrow alleyways to reach imposing churches and broad plazas.**

There is very little evidence that almost 600 years have passed since the founding of the Real Villa, the royal town of Teguise. Maciot de Béthencourt built the first colonial town on the Canary Islands in 1428, on the site of an even older Majo settlement, and named it after his wife, a Majo princess. Teguise remained the capital of the island until 1852. Powerful families, such as the Herreras and Feo Perazas, built their townhouses here.

But why up there so far from the coast? This is a good question, as cool trade winds blow through the streets, clouds often shroud the town in mist and it is always cooler than by the sea. But the early inhabitants had good reason to choose this settlement. During the winter the vital rain falling on the neighbouring mountain of Guanapay was collected in a giant underground cistern, the *Gran Mareta*. Furthermore, the Spanish colonials felt safer away from the coast given the threat of pirate attacks. The protection offered by the powerful castle, the Castillo Santa Bárbara built nearby on the Guanapay, gave added protection.

But they were wrong. Teguise was repeatedly attacked from the sea. A plaque in the *Callejón de Sangre* ("Blood Alley") behind the Church of Nuestra Señora de Guadalupe recalls a massacre carried out by the feared Algerian buccaneers in 1586. In 1618 pirates burned the place to the ground, so the oldest surviving buildings date from the 17th century. But that doesn't take anything away from their splendour. The historic centre of the town with its unique architectural style has been under a preservation order since 1973.

Now Teguise leads a double life. The atmosphere on weekdays is relaxed. Locals as well as the many foreigners who live here sit next to the odd daytripper or two at one of the stylish or trendy cafés before they browse through the nice shops. But on Sunday the place comes alive and almost bursts at the seams for market day. The *mercadillo* here is one of Lanzarote's main attractions. Holidaymakers arrive in buses in their thousands; countless traders, here to peddle kitsch and knick-knacks from all over the world, also descend on the town. Folk groups are on hand

SIGHTSEEING

CASTILLO SANTA BÁRBARA

The small but solid fortress on the Guanapay volcano outside Teguise is visible from some distance. It can be reached

Half the island comes to Teguise for the Sunday market

to entertain the throngs of visitors. The streets and the squares, the whole town in fact, resembles an oriental bazaar. In the bars shoppers jostle for drinks, which are often much dearer on that day than elsewhere on the island. The Gran Mareta, the rather forlorn plaza above the ancient cisterns behind the church, is jam-packed with takeaway food stalls. Although all the bustle has very little to do with day-to-day life on the island, the *mercadillo* is something to behold, as there is nothing quite so hectic and chaotic anywhere else on Lanzarote. And then by Sunday evening Teguise has returned to its slumbers.

via a tarmac road, which branches off to the right from the road to Haría at the town edge. This fortress was built in the 16th century to protect the islanders from pirate attacks. Sometimes up to 1000 people sought refuge within its walls.

The entrance is a separate stone staircase with drawbridge. Initially a museum documenting emigration from the Canary Islands was housed there, but with the recent re-emergence of piracy on the high seas, the castle has become the *Museo de la Piratería (daily 10am–4pm | admission 3 euros | www.museodelapirateria.com)*. Take the opportunity to go up onto the ☀ roof for a magnificent view over the northern half of the island.

A proud lion keeps watch over the Plaza de la Constitución in Teguise with its church

LA CILLA

This former tithe house, built in the 17th century, was the collecting point for the corn tax, which Lanzarote had to pay to the bishop on Gran Canaria. Now it houses a large arts and crafts shop.

CONVENTO DE SAN FRANCISCO

Look instead of pray: a museum of sacred art has now taken up residence in the former convent church. Dramatically staged, expressive sculptures of saints are everywhere. The architecture is also worth a closer look: the ornate wooden ceilings soaring above the naves are simply breathtaking! *Tue–Sat 9:30am–4:30pm, Sun 10am–2pm | admission 2 euros | Plaza San Francisco*

CONVENTO DE SANTO DOMINGO

Art in a church can also be viewed in this former Dominican monastery. Magnificent wooden ceilings, whitewashed walls and a showy, colourful rococo altar form the backdrop for changing exhibitions. *Sun–Fri 10am–3pm | admission 1.50 euros*

GRAN MARETA

This cistern, once the largest on Lanzarote, was built to store rainwater. Later it silted up. When the desalination plants were commissioned, it was surplus to requirements and was concreted over. Now the broad plaza behind the church is used to stage outdoor events and as space for the Sunday market.

IGLESIA DE NUESTRA SEÑORA DE GUADALUPE

Your place to find some peace and quiet if you have come to the busy Sunday market. This parish church on the Plaza de la Constitución was consecrated in the 15th century, destroyed by pirates in 1680, then subsequently rebuilt. It is dedicated to Our Lady of Guadalupe, who is revered in Spain and in South America.

Inside the bright naves, the colourfully painted figures of saints will catch your eye. The impressive façade with its huge stone tower contributes to the beautiful atmosphere on the plaza.

PALACIO MARQUÉS DE HERRERA Y ROJAS

This rather nondescript palace (1455) has a fine, covered inner courtyard. An exhibition of pieces made by the local craft school occupies the vestibule. Admission is free, but not all rooms are open to the public. *Mon–Fri 8am–3pm | C/ José Betancort*

PALACIO DE SPÍNOLA/CASA-MUSEO DEL TIMPLE ●

A house for nobility with a surprising interior: The prized gem in old Teguise is this old palace on the plaza, built between 1730 and 1780. Particularly impressive are the courtyards, the chapel and the original kitchen. But even more impressive is the timple museum housed in the stately rooms of the Palacio de Spínola. Stringed instruments from around the world related to the Canarian timple (a five-stringed instrument resembling a ukulele) are on display and their sounds fill the rooms. A workshop is set up to show just how much work goes into making these instruments. Once in a while, INSIDER TIP masters of the timple play concerts for the public. *Mon–Sat 9am–4:30pm, Sun 9am–3:30pm | admission 3 euros | www.casadeltimple.org*

PLAZA DE LA CONSTITUCIÓN ★

Around the central square in Teguise are some of the finest examples of colonial architecture: the Iglesia de Nuestra Señora de Guadalupe, the former La Cilla grain store and the Palacio de Spínola guarded by two lions. The palm and laurel trees provide some shade.

FOOD & DRINK

ACATIFE

A classic among Lanzarote's restaurants in a venerable building. Traditional, hearty fare. Try the rabbit in red wine sauce *(conejo al vino tinto)*! *Closed Mon | C/ San Miguel 4 | tel. 928 84 50 37 | Moderate*

BODEGA SANTA BÁRBARA

Wine and snacks served in the mini-patio of this small bodega, inside more dishes. A mouth-watering range of tapas in the display cabinet. *Closed Sat | C/ La Cruz 5 | tel. 928 59 48 41 | Moderate*

LA CANTINA

Rich in tradition, this "canteen" in a historic house dishes up Canarian home-style cooking with a twist. It often plays host to live bands at the weekend. *Tue–Sat noon–11pm, Sun 10am–6pm | C/ León y Castillo 8 | mobile tel. 6 20 85 60 64 | www.cantinateguise.com | Budget–Moderate*

HESPÉRIDES ◉

Located in an old townhouse, this small restaurant serves organic ingredients from the Demeter store across the street. The speciality of chef Dailos Airam is the traditional Lanzarote dish *mini-truchas con calabaza* (dough pockets with a pumpkin filling). But the other choices are nothing to be ashamed of either and certainly worth a try! Vegetarians will love the tasty salads. *Closed Sun evening | C/ León y Castillo 3 | tel. 928 59 40 12 | www.biohesperides.blogspot.com | Moderate*

IKARUS

You can dine on unique tapas and enjoy good island wine at this gastro bar on the atmospheric square. A salsa band plays in the courtyard during the Sunday market. *Daily from 9am | Plaza Clavijo y Fajardo 6 | tel. 928 84 57 01 | Moderate*

SHOPPING

Teguise has always been an important centre of Canarian culture. And in recent years more and more artists and artisans from northern Europe have moved to the island. The town's shops stock a large selection of crafts, jewellery and paintings.

LA LONJA EXCLUSIVA

This small shop sells approved copies of works by César Manrique. *Plaza de 18 de Julio*

MERCADILLO

The large Sunday market is the perfect place for browsers. Here you can find everything from art and arty knickknacks to day-to-day items such as second-hand clothing, shoes and fresh fruit. Also on sale are many 🌐 delicious forms of farm produce: *chorizo,* the piquant pork sausage with dried red peppers, or *turrón,* a nougat dessert in many different variations. Buses leave from the holiday centres and Arrecife, charges payable for parking on the edge of the town. *Sun 9am–2pm*

TIMPLE WORKSHOP
ANTONIO LEMES HERNÁNDEZ ⬤

Antonio Lemes Hernández is one of the last craftsmen making the famous Canarian guitar, the timple. For almost all his life he has been in his workshop piecing together the parts for about 15 different instruments of varying sizes, from the mini-timple to the contra-timple, a month. A beautiful but expensive souvenir. The standard instrument costs around 200 euros, more elaborate models with pearl inlays and marquetry 400–500 euros. *C/ Flores 8*

WHERE TO STAY

FINCA MALVARROSA

Former farmhouse with two apartments within easy walking distance from the centre. Both are furnished attractively in rustic style. Amenities include kitchen, bathroom, terrace and swimming pool. *C/ Malvarrosa 41 | tel. 928 59 30 17 | www.fincamalvarrosa.com | Moderate*

INFORMATION

Plaza de la Constitución (tel. 928 84 53 98 | www.turismoteguise.com)

WHERE TO GO

ERMITA DE LAS NIEVES ✷
(129 D1) (*𝄡 G7*)

This whitewashed pilgrimage chapel stands high up on the Risco de Famara. The chapel is dedicated to the Virgen de las Nievas or Our Lady of the Snows, who has over the years received countless pleas for rain to fall on Lanzarote. Although the chapel is usually closed (mass Sat 5pm), the long climb is worth the effort, if only to see one of the INSIDER TIP finest panoramic views on the island. The cliffs drop almost vertically 600 m (1960 ft) into the sea. The islands of La Graciosa and Montaña Clara, the Playa de Famara, Teguise and the Timanfaya volcanoes are clearly visible.

HARÍA ★ (125 D5) (*𝄡 G6*)

When suddenly you descend into the valley of a thousand palms at the foot of the Famara Mountains, the scene is more Africa than Europe. Countless broad-crowned Canarian palms stand proudly among the low, white houses. Haría (pop. 5000) is the friendliest place on Lanzarote. It is where you will see how lanzaroteños used to live. So no surprise

A Virgin of the Snow with a premium view: you can see the ocean behind the Ermita de las Nieves

then that in his old age César Manrique retired to Haría and is buried here. His house, a traditional Lanzarote-style residence, is open to the public. It seems as if César Manrique himself has just left the rooms and the atelier in the *Casa Museo César Manrique (daily 10:30am–2:30pm | C/ Elvira Sánchez 30 | admission 10 euros | www.fcmanrique.org)*.

Take a stroll through the village to discover old villas with luxuriant patios, small shops and bars. The *Plaza León y Castillo* with its shady weeping fig trees opens out in front of the church and is the perfect place for a break. The small *Museo Sacro Popular* on the square near the church displays sacred sculptures and paintings, but it is only open during the Saturday market.

Women gather in the *Taller Municipal de Artesanía* craft centre *(summer Mon–Sat 10am–1pm and 3pm–5pm, winter 10am–3pm and 4pm–6pm)* near the Plaza de la Constitución to work on embroidery and shawls in keeping with the old tradition. These labour-intensive goods are sold on the INSIDER TIP *Saturday market (mercadillo)* and you will see many more artisans selling their wares here too. Also on sale here are home-made speciality food and drinks, e.g. ❂ organic goat's cheese from Haría. Temporary exhibitions are held in the *El Aljibe* gallery *(Mon–Sat 10am–3pm)*, formerly the water reservoir beneath the Plaza de la Constitución. A good place for a coffee is *La Sociedad Bar Tegala (daily | tel. 6 96 90 06 52 | Budget)* on the shady plaza. The best place to eat is ❂ INSIDER TIP *Puerta Verde (daily 1pm–10pm | C/ Fajardo 24 | tel. 9 28 83 53 50 | Moderate)*: The pasta, ice cream and cakes are all home-made and the dishes are seasoned with fresh herbs from the garden. Stay in one of the two nice apartments of the small finca ☀ INSIDER TIP *Casita de la Abuela*

A signpost that's like an exclamation mark – typical Manrique

(C/ Vista La Vega 22 | tel. 6 29 53 22 25 | www.lanzarote-abseits-tourismus.com | Moderate) with a far-reaching view over the valley of palms.

INSIDER TIP LAGOMAR (129 D3) (*M* F8)

Hidden away in a former quarry in is this eccentric, fortress-like estate. Its first owner, in the Seventies, was the actor Omar Sharif, of *Dr Zhivago* fame, who is said to have gambled it away in a game of bridge...

Now the place is home to, among other things, a *Museum (Tue–Sun 10am–6pm | admission 6 euros):* You can walk through caves and tunnels, set at different levels around an artificial pond, as you pass the Sharif Room. On display here are posters recalling the great actor's heyday; there is even a photo of that fateful card game. During the day, the *Café-Restaurant (closed Mon | Budget–Moderate)* serves tapas and daily specials, but in the evening upmarket Mediterranean cuisine takes over. An upscale lounge ambiance prevails in the cave bar *La Cueva (closed Mon).* After 8pm, refined lighting and sound ef-

fects make for a magical evening. Additionally, two modern ☼ *apartments (tel. 9 28 84 54 60 | Expensive)* are set into the rock. Amenities include a terrace and pool plus a sweeping view over Lanzarote's central plain. *C/ Los Loros 6 | 9 28 84 56 65 | www.lag-o-mar.com*

MIRADOR DE GUINATE ● ☼
(125 D4) (*M* G5)

The view from the Mirador de Guinate near the village of the same name is no less spectacular than the view from the Mirador del Río (see below) – but free.

MIRADOR DEL RÍO ★ ☼
(125 E3) (*M* G4–5)

Stunning is the only word to describe the view from this former fortification, the Batería del Río, perched precariously on a cliff top at a height of 479 m (1570 ft) in the far north of Lanzarote. The view extends as far as the islands of La Graciosa and Alegranza. Dating from 1974, the mirador complex was one of César Man-

rique's first works. It fits perfectly into the environment. *Daily 10am–5:45pm | admission 4.50 euros*

PLAYA DE FAMARA
(124–125 C–D 5–6) (*Ø F–G6*)
Famara beach is the longest on Lanzarote and scenically one of the finest. It runs below the rugged Famara Mountains, bordered on one side by dunes and on the other by the crashing waves of the Atlantic. There's often a strong wind blowing, so pay attention to the beach safety flag. If it's red, it means positively no swimming. Every year the dangerous currents claim lives.

The *Playa Famara* bungalow complex *(50 apartments | tel. 928 84 51 32 | www.bungalowsplayafamara.com | Moderate)* may have lost some of its initial sheen, but the complex occupies a stunning location on the mountainside.

A popular spot for surfers and a hideaway for those wishing to shun mass tourism is *La Caleta de Famara*. There are several bars and restaurants here. Surfers often take breakfast in the *Croissantería (daily | Budget)*. For the best view, try the ☼ *Restaurante El Risco (closed Mon | C/ Montaña Clara 36 | tel. 928 52 85 50 | www.restauranteelrisco.com | Expensive)*, which once belonged to a brother of César Manrique. It is now in the hands of a different proprietor and has been smartened up. What remains is the blue and white paint, the magnificent panorama of the Famara cliffs and the ever-present sound of crashing ocean waves.

The ⊕ INSIDER TIP *El Sibarita (closed Mon | Av. El Marinero 128 | on the western edge of town | tel. 928 52 85 31 | Budget–Moderate)* is all about healthy and affordable food: Lipez and Eduardo serve vegan and vegetarian dishes in trendy ambience. The menu includes quinoa schnitzel and tofu burgers, fantastic salads and gofio crêpes with cactus jam – everything can be ordered to go. Also (organic) wines from the island and a selection of herbal teas to finish up the meal.

Water as smooth as glass in front of a craggy cliff: the spectacular Famara Beach

PUERTO DEL CARMEN AND THE CENTRE

The bright green vine grows in a pit about 2 m/6.6 ft deep, surrounded by a layered, semi-circular wall of grey stone. The soil is black, and the green leaves stand out starkly against the dark background; the vine could almost be a cheap plastic imitation.

But this is not some crazy idea dreamed up by a small-scale gardener; what you see is skilfully worked farmland on which grapes are grown commercially. Thousands of vines, each with its own small crater, cower under the harsh conditions, a dry stone wall offering scant protection. The vine-growing region extends across this lowland strip like a work by a graphic designer; it's so unreal that the New York Museum of Modern Art devoted a special exhibition to this bizarre landscape. But

can the farmers get the vines to grow using such unusual methods?

Yes, they can and it's actually very successful. To ripen the grapes in this dust-dry climate with its strong trade winds, countless tiny grains of lava – for that is what the soil consists of – are essential components. Being porous, the lapilli, as they are known, absorb moisture from the onshore wind which at night blows over La Geria – the word means wind-break – and then during the day the accumulated water gradually drips down into the roots of the vines. Only using this unique form of cultivation is it possible to bring the fruits to maturity. The result of what is known as *enarenado* cultivation can be seen – and sampled – between Uga and Masdache. Along the

Photo: Wine cultivation in a lava field near La Geria

The green of the vines contrasts strangely with the black soil, creating a man-made landscape that is unique on the planet

country road there are many bodegas, where the aroma of earthy wine wafts up from the cellars. The traditional Malvasia grape is now being replaced more and more by other vine varieties, which yield a drier, lighter wine. But the wine of Lanzarote can never deny its origins. While their red wines compare poorly with those from mainland Spain, the lanzaroteños make a beautifully fresh white wine, a fine accompaniment to fish dishes and the powerful Canarian sauces. Tourism dominates the southern coastal zone in Lanzarote's central area, particularly around Puerto del Carmen. The former farming villages of Machér, Tías and San Bartolomé have grown dramatically in recent decades and are nice enough places, but have no particular attractions. To the north of La Geria however, as far as the coast between La Santa and Sóo, old traditions linger among the people and on the land. The deliciously fruity tomatoes and the searingly hot onions, which add character to the local *ensalada mixta,* come from these parts. Also grown in this

How was the catch? There's not a fish in sight on the boats at Puerto del Carmen

part of the island is a type of baby potato which stays firm when boiled. Known as *papas arrugadas,* you see them on the menu in restaurants serving local specialities. They have a distinctive wrinkly skin. The region around Mancha Blanca and Tinajo is still firmly in the hands of the farming community. The fields are divided into neat plots and the green and white villages are in good shape. Tall candelabra trees *(euphorbia ingens)* and poinsettias grow in their carefully tended gardens. There is no mistaking the fact that tourism has brought money to the island. Until the 1970s the rural areas suffered from grinding poverty.

Happily, the receipts from tourism have played a large part in maintaining this region's cultural heritage. The church of the island's patron saint, Nuestra Señora de los Volcanes, has been restored to its former splendour in gleaming white on the edge of the village of Mancha Blanca. And the old farming estate, which now hosts one of the best private museums in

the Canary Islands, the Museo Agrícola El Patio in Tiagua, would now probably be no more than an abandoned ruin.

PUERTO DEL CARMEN

MAP INSIDE THE BACK COVER
(131 F4) *(M D10)* **The former fishing village Puerto del Carmen (pop. 3000) has blossomed into a top-class tourist centre. The village divides up into an older quarter around the fishing harbour and a vast expanse of holiday villages with 35,000 beds in the north.** The main reason behind the rapid development of this small town into a major resort is the splendid beaches blessed with clean water. Above them, the traffic-reduced *Avenida de las Playas* stretches for 7 km (4 miles) along the coast. While the eye glories in the green of the palms and the yellow of

the sand towards the coast, inland, it is met by a sheer endless chain of bars and restaurants, arcades and smaller shopping centres. If one long party on the promenade is not for you, head for the upper town or seek out one of the big hotels facing away from the road. There you can enjoy your holiday undisturbed.

Puerto del Carmen has something for everyone. In the old town by the fishing harbour, the everyday life of the locals takes centre-stage. Just as they have done for centuries, the fishermen will be out in the morning by their boats sorting through last night's catch. Throughout the day there always seems to be a few anglers whiling away their time on the quayside and in the evening groups of men armed with metal balls assemble for a round of pétanque. And if mass is about to start in the small chapel, Nuestra Señora del Carmen, which you can hardly find among all the fish restaurants, the faithful are spilling out on the street – locals and visitors alike.

FOOD & DRINK

Tourist hotspot Puerto del Carmen claims to have more than 200 restaurants. But not all of them are recommended. Many, particularly along Avenida de las Playas, are interested only in a rapid turnover. If you want original Canarian dishes, perhaps with locally caught fish, it's better to look around the fishing harbour.

EL ANCLA

This new building made from red and grey volcanic blocks is just a little too flashy here, in the harbour quarter. But the tapas are always beautifully presented. Large awnings cover the terrace opposite the pétanque piste, where the men gather to enjoy their favourite pas-

time. *Daily | tel. 928 51 36 39 | Budget–Moderate*

BLOOMING CACTUS ☺

Greek-inspired tapas hit the tables at this vegetarian-vegan bistro above the harbour – healthy, fresh and tasty! *Tue–Sun from 6pm | C/ Teide 35 | tel. 6 08 29 38 37 | www.bloomingcactus.co.uk | Budget*

BOZENA'S

The pleasant ambiance in this faux-antique house above the harbour is enchanting. As are the dishes prepared by the Polish-Irish couple Bozena and Deco. To satisfy your sweet tooth, order the Polish apple cake *(szarlotka)* or the

MARCO POLO HIGHLIGHTS

⭐ **Los Jameos Playa**
Hotel in Puerto del Carmen, managed to environmental standards, designed in Canarian style and with the beach right on the doorstep → p. 67

⭐ **La Geria**
In what is probably the world's most unusual wine-growing region, plenty of bodegas invite you to taste the local wines → p. 68

⭐ **Casa Museo del Campesino**
The "House of the Farmer" is inspired by traditional architecture. And artisans are busy in the workshops → p. 69

⭐ **Museo Agrícola El Patio**
The island's farming history lives on here: Dromedaries pull the plough, the bodega looks like it did 100 years ago → p. 71

Irish Bailey's cheesecake! *Mon–Sat from 6:30pm | C/ Teide 6 | tel. 928 51 14 63 | Budget–Moderate*

CASA ROJA

There's hardly a better way of watching the sun go down – the perfect place for a romantic meal. You sit on a long and narrow terrace a few metres above the

MARDELEVA

Although quiet, this restaurant still has a view of the sea thanks to its hidden location above the harbour. Enjoy tasty fish dishes, solid tapas and Lanzarote wines as the fresh Atlantic breeze brushes your skin. *Daily from 10:30am | C/ los Infantes 10 | tel. 928 51 06 86 | Moderate*

Something for romantics: a dinner under a sea of lights on the terrace of the Casa Roja

water in the old harbour basin. *Daily | Av. del Varadero 22 | tel. 928 51 07 03 | Moderate*

COFRADÍA DE PESCADORES LA TIÑOSA

The fishermen always bring their catches to their cooperative *(cofradía)* first. The fish are cleaned and gutted right before the tables on the terrace and then fried *a la plancha* (on a hot plate). You can't get any closer to the boats as they come and go. *Daily | Plaza del Varadero | tel. 6 60 43 35 78 | Moderate*

TASTE OF INDIA

Fancy something more exotic? Almost at the northern tip of the promenade (near Hotel Jameos Playa), you can dine Indian-style with a sea view. Good curries, Chicken Tikka and Lamb Jalfrezi plus an inexpensive lunch menu! *Daily noon–11pm | C. C. Los Jameos, Local 33 | tel. 928 51 62 54 | www.facebook.com/ tasteofindialanzarote | Moderate*

TERRAZA PLAYA

The terrace with just a handful of tables right by rocks occasionally splashed by the sea gives this restaurant a special appeal. A large menu with plenty of fish and meat dishes to choose from. *Daily | Av de las Playas 28 | tel. 928 515 417 | Moderate*

INSIDER TIP VINO + LANZAROTE

First, there was only a wine and gourmet foods shop, but then the visitors kept wanting to sample all of the delicacies on site. And so Ms Hanneke and Señor Miguel opened a tapas bar next door where they offer the best wines of the island, served by the glass, together with delicious tapas – from deep-fried eggplant with palm honey to Iberian ham. Live music is featured twice a week – be sure to make a reservation! *Closed Sun | C/ Timanfaya s/n, C.C. Playa Blanca L. 14 | tel. 928 516 959 | Budget*

SHOPPING

BIOSFERA PLAZA

For shopaholics: you will find many Spanish-made products at the small but chic shopping centre made of chrome and glass: fashions from Blanco, Bershka, Sfera and Zara, leather accessories from Piel de Toro and cosmetics from Aloe Plus. *Av. Juan Carlos I 15 | above the harbour | www.biosferaplaza.es*

EL NIÑO

Surf shop with a wide range of water sports equipment and sportswear from all the top brands. *Av. de las Playas 35*

BEACHES

The more fool you if you don't test the waters at Puerto del Carmen! Of the local beaches, the very best is the more than 1-km long *Playa Blanca* (a.k.a. *Playa Grande)*, situated at the foot of low cliffs and dotted with shady palms. This beach is followed to the east by the even longer and less busy *Playa de los Pocillos* and *Playa Matagorda*. You can rent loungers and umbrellas on all three beaches, and emergency services are also available. Small but nice is the *Playa de la Barrilla,* near the harbour below the former town centre. Two rocky ridges flank this beach of fine sand. As long as the normal trade winds are blowing, the currents at these beaches are mostly gentle and the wind and waves not very strong. This means that, in general, the waters are not dangerous for swimming – even for children.

LEISURE & SPORTS

Is there anything more enjoyable to do on an island than take a boat trip? The water bus sails several times a day to the neighbouring coastal city of Puerto Calero *(6 euros one way | www.lineas romero.com/lineas/waterbuspcarmen*

LOW BUDGET

In Puerto del Carmen, leaflets granting free admission or discounts for theme parks or the casino are often distributed in the hotels. So keep your eyes open!

Check out the basic *Pensión Magec (12 rooms | C/ Hierro 11 | tel. 928 515 120 | www.pensionmagec. com)* in the old quarter. Double rooms start at 30 euros.

● Loungers on the playas in Puerto del Carmen are free from 5pm – and you'll still get another two hours of sun.

pcalero).The yacht *Maype* can be booked for one to six-hour boat trips *(incl. snorkelling tours and lunch, from 30 euros | www.seafunlanzarote.com)*. Adrenaline junkies can take to the air. You are attached to both a parachute and a line on a speedboat *(Paracraft Lanzarote | 50 euros/10 min. | Paseo de la Barilla | tel. 928 51 26 61 | www.watersports-lanzarote.com)*. The Flyboard costs twice as much; a lot cheaper are the jet boat, banana boat and crazy UFO.

ENTERTAINMENT

Start off your evening on the town at the old harbour and then head out to the Avenida de las Playas.

AMERICAN INDIAN CAFÉ
Disco and cocktail bar for 30- to 50-year-olds with live shows and video clips on screens. *Daily 10am–3am | Av. de las Playas 35 | www.american-indian-cafe.com*

CASINO
The roulette wheels and slot machines never stop spinning at the oceanfront casino – this may be your chance to fill up your holiday piggy bank. Don't forget your identity card! *Daily 4pm–4am | admission 3 euros | Av. de las Playas 12 | www.grancasinolanzarote.com*

GOLDEN CORNER
A quiet place to relax and popular among people aged 30 or over for its large selection of cocktails. *Daily from 10pm | Av. de la Playas 16*

INSIDER TIP THE ISLAND LIVE MUSIC BAR
International singers and songwriters give concerts above the old harbour and the audience moves to the music! *Fri–Wed from 8pm | C/ Tenerife | www.islandbarlanzarote.com*

LA OLA ●
Although "the wave" is open during the day, it is at its best in the evening when the red lighting accentuates the Moroccan-inspired interior. Relax on a Bali lounger above the sea or smoke a water pipe in the pavilion! *Daily from 10am | Av. de las Playas 10 | www.cafelaola.com*

RUTA 66
This large disco/pub is the hottest spot in Puerto del Carmen. Opens out on to the promenade. Several bars, football on wide screens and dancing to US rock. *Daily from 10pm | Centro Comercial Arena Dorada | Av. de las Playas*

STARLIGHT CINEMA
Watching a movie under the stars: English-language films are shown almost every evening on the rooftop terrace of the Biosfera Plaza shopping centre. There are no seats; instead, you just lie back and order some drinks and snacks. *Daily 6:30pm and 8:45pm | C.C. Biosfera Plaza (5th level) | Av. Juan Carlos 15 | www.rooftopbiosfera.com*

WHERE TO STAY

INSIDER TIP CENTRO DE TERAPIA ANTROPOSÓFICA
Feel like spending your holiday at a hotel with a personal touch, a place to unwind, a place to do something for your health and be creative? Far above the hustle and bustle of the tourist centre of Puerto del Carmen, this small complex has simple but beautiful apartments clustered around an exotic pool garden. Physicians, massage therapists and physical therapists at the treatment centre address your individual needs. You can relax in the

Get into the mood with ice-cold cocktails. This is what holiday tastes like

34°C/93.2°F "floating pool", try out workshops for painting and sculpting and enjoy classical music concerts. The buffet includes a wide selection of vegetarian options and there is an 🌿 organic supermarket in the city for self-caterers. However, anyone who really wants to get away from it all should make a reservation at the 🌿 organic *Finca de los Lomos,* which is only a few minutes' drive away and offers 17 holiday apartments. *52 apartments | C/ Salinas 12 | tel. 9 28 51 28 42 | www.centro-lanzarote.de/ en/seite.php | Moderate*

LAS COSTAS

This complex right by the Playa de los Pocillos has undergone a total refit and become an extravagantly glazed, cool and ultra-modern hotel. *187 rooms | Av. de las Playas 88 | tel. 928 51 43 46 | www. hibiscus-hotels.com | Moderate*

SUITEHOTEL FARIONES PLAYA

The overbearing façade of dark lava rock is not to everyone's taste. But inside the beautifully designed gardens, which open towards the sea, are much admired. *231 rooms | C/ Acatife 1 | tel. 928 51 34 00 | www.farioneshotels.com | Moderate*

LOS JAMEOS PLAYA ⭐ 🌿

This large and convivial hotel is both family-friendly and, because it operates energy-saving systems, environmentally friendly. This warm atmosphere is evident as soon as you enter the entrance lobby overlooked by wooden balconies in traditional Canarian style. The bright rooms are furnished with wooden furniture and the Pocillos beach is on the doorstep. *530 rooms | C/ de Marte 2 | tel. 928 511717 | www.los-jameos-playa.de | Moderate–Expensive*

SAN ANTONIO

This traditional four-star is one of the few hotels that can rightly claim to be **INSIDER TIP** by the sea, namely the broad Playa de los Pocillos. Many of the rooms have a view over the sea toward Fuerteventura; large freshwater and seawater pools in the subtropical garden, plus glazed sauna with view of the heavens. Excellent buffets changing daily, shows in the evening, tennis courts, casual atmosphere. *331 rooms | Av. de las Playas 84 | tel. 928 51 42 00 | www.vikho tels.com | Moderate–Expensive*

INFORMATION

Av. de las Playas (Playa Grande | tel. 928 51 33 51 | www.puertodelcarmen.com)

WHERE TO GO

LA GERIA ★
(127 D–F 4–5) (*ф C–E 9–10*)
The countryside around La Geria could be mistaken for the work of a brilliant landscape architect. The main route through the region runs from Mozaga in the centre of the island via Masdache as far as Uga in the south. The awesome vine region near the volcanic mountains appears to be even more intensively farmed when approached from the minor roads, such as from the road to La Vegueta. What is hard to believe is that nature itself initially brought new life to the barren land in the form of the delicate, grey-green lichen. Only much, much later did farmers move into vegetable and fruit growing, creating new plots of arable land.

The main bodegas are beside the main road, most of them opening from 10:30am to 6pm. The *El Grifo* winery *(LZ 30, km 11 | tel. 928 52 40 36 | www. elgrifo.com)* has a wine museum *(admission 4 euros)* where tools, some of which are over 200 years old, are exhibited. The *Bodegas Barreto (LZ 30, km 11 | tel. 928 52 07 17)* offer a wide selection of wines from 7 to 9 euros (tasting included). The bodega *Stratvs (LZ 30, km*

18 | closed temporarily at the time of publication) looks like a cathedral built into the mountain.

The ☆ *Bodega La Geria (LZ 30, km 19) | tel. 928 17 31 78 | www.lageria.com)* is situated directly opposite a fine dragon tree. If you take a tour through the *Bodegas Rubicón (LZ 30, km 19) | tel. 928 17 37 08 | www.bodegasrubicon.com)*, a restored historic house, you will be shown the beautiful wine cellar and old presses before you can sample the wines. This rather primitive bodega is a little out of the way, accessible via a rough track: ● ☆ *El Chupadero (LZ 30, km 18.8) | tel. 928 17 31 15 | www.el-chupadero.com | Moderate)* offers a cosy tapas bar with a terrace where you can unhurriedly snack on Mediterranean delicacies and sip the house wines. There is a view over thousands of mini-craters cradling the precious vines.

MANCHA BLANCA (127 D–E3) (*ф D8*)
In 1735 streams of lava poured out of the Timanfaya volcanoes and advanced relentlessly on the little village. In desperation the inhabitants made one final attempt to avert the imminent catastrophe: they placed a statue of the village patron saint, Nuestra Señora de los Dolores, in front of the glowing lava as it edged ever closer. And it worked. The molten lava came to a standstill right in front of the figure. By way of thanks, the villagers built the church Iglesia de los Dolores on the edge of the village and proclaimed the Madonna to be Señora de los Volcanes – Our Lady of the Volcanoes. She then became the island's patron saint. On the road to Timanfaya National Park, you will pass the *Visitor Centre* (see p. 75).

MOZAGA (128 B3–4) (*ф E8*)
On the roundabout outside this village stands one of Manrique's largest pieces, the *Monumento al Campesino*, the Peas-

ants' Monument. It was built at the end of the 1960s to draw attention to the worsening plight of the farmers. Appropriately it comprises water tanks from old fishing boats boats stacked together into a large, Cubist-inspired dromedary. It serves as a reminder that the island does not have an inexhaustible supply of resources.

928 52 01 36 | *Moderate)* in lava vaults, serving typical Lanzarotean dishes. In the cosier bar on the ground floor you can sit on a gleaming white terrace, view the *monumento* and eat Lanzarotean tapas. The Béthencourt family run the **INSIDER TIP** *Caserío de Mozaga (6 rooms | C/ Malva 8 | tel. 928 52 00 60 | www. ca-*

A dromedary on a roundabout? Manrique's water tank installation lets your imagination take flight

Nearby is the ⭐ *Casa Museo del Campesino (daily 10am–5:45pm | admission free),* a farmers' and arts and crafts museum where you can watch craftsmen and women at work and purchase their products. As well as watching embroiderers and weavers (only occasionally) at work, the activities in the pottery workshop are of special interest. The artisans here make *novios de mojón:* originally, these clay figure couples with their exaggerated sexual organs were made by the early inhabitants as fertility symbols and given to young couples.

The lower part of the old farmhouse houses a restaurant *(daily | tel.*

seriodemozaga.com | Moderate) in a grand 18th-century country house. At this delightful hotel you'll feel right at home and have no trouble getting to know the other guests.

PLAYA QUEMADA (131 D4) *(ᗰ C11)*
A translation of quemada is "burnt", a reference to the fact that the beach here is black and stony. There are a few houses and one or two Canarian restaurants, but apart from that, there's little here to detain you. For this reason, however, it appeals to holidaymakers seeking peace and quiet. Beyond the rocky crest, which is flooded at high tide, there is

another beach that's never crowded. If you would like to linger and explore the craggy coastline, try the offerings at the *Restaurante Salmarina (Av. Marítima 13 | tel. 928 17 35 62 | www.salmarinarestaurante.com | Moderate)*. Sit here right by the water in a part-maritime, part-rustic ambience and enjoy good quality fish and seafood without any frills.

PUERTO CALERO (131 E4) (*ɯ D10*)

Many sailors stop off here on their way from Europe to America. Even if you are not an ocean-going mariner, it is worth a visit. It is fun to stroll along the very elegant seafront promenade with its golden bollards and row of blue and white houses. Sailing trips including five-hour catamaran tours depart from here *(daily 11am–3:30pm | 59–64 euros | tel. 928 51 30 22 | www.catlanza.com)*. Another option is a descent to the sea-bed in a submarine: ● *Submarine Safaris (dives 10am, 11am, noon, 2pm | 55 eu-*

ros, online reductions | tel. 928 51 28 89 | www.submarinesafaris.com).
The noble **INSIDER TIP** *Restaurant Amura (daily | tel. 928 51 31 81 | www.restauranteamura.com | Expensive)* was designed in the style of a Southern-state villa with a large veranda and palm terrace. Located at the end of the marina it serves imaginative fusion dishes. The four-star hotel *Costa Calero (324 rooms | tel. 928 84 95 95 | www.hotelcostacalero.com | Expensive)*, minimalist in style and finished in Mediterranean colours, is renowned for its great buffets and wide range of activities. The thermal indoor pool in the ● Roman-inspired spa extends deep into the garden. Other facilities include bike hire and diving equipment.

SAN BARTOLOMÉ (128 B4) (*ɯ E9*)

A plaza with a church, the town hall and a theatre make this quiet municipality a pleasant place. Kitty-corner to the square,

Set sail and dock: even without a sailboat the yacht harbour of Puerto Calero is a popular place

the house with striking murals is the private *Museo Etnográfico Tanit (Mon–Sat 10am–2pm | admission 6 euros | C/ Constitución 1 | www.museotanit.com)* with its lovingly-created displays of artefacts, including tools, furniture, toys, clothes and costumes from days gone by. A few steps further on, the historic *Casa Cerdeña* houses the *Tourist Office (C/ Doctor Cerdeña Bethencourt 17 | tel. 9 28 52 23 51)*. Book-lovers trek to the town of Tías, 7 km (4.3 miles) to the southwest, where the finca of the Nobel prize-winning author José Saramago, who died in 2010, has been turned into a museum called *A Casa José Saramago (Mon–Sat 10am–2:30pm, tours every 30 minutes | admission 8 euros | C/ Los Topes 2 | Tías | tel. 9 28 83 35 26 | www.acasajosesaramago.com).*

LA SANTA (127 E1) (𝄞 D7)

Every serious athlete has heard of this little hamlet on the northern coast. It is home to the training oasis *La Santa (tel. Mon–Fri 9am–5pm | www.clublaasanta.com/en)*, a club that offers dozens of sporting activities and has its own athletics stadium, windsurfing lagoon, and road cycling base. For regular day trippers, the nondescript town has little to offer other than a multitude of restaurants along the through road. The *Alma Tapas (closed Mon. | Av. Marinero 26 | Moderate)* serves excellent snacks and daily specials in a pretty courtyard.

TIAGUA (127 F3) (𝄞 E8)

You would probably drive right by the farming village if it weren't for the ★ *Museo Agrícola El Patio (Mon–Fri 10am–5pm, Sat 10am–2:30pm | admission 5 euros including a small sample of wine)*. The museum is housed in an old, but well-preserved farmhouse and provides a glimpse into the traditions of the peasants. All the displays, from the bodega to the gofio mill, are in full working order. Chicken are roaming about in the garden, goats bleat from the stables, and in the shade, a dromedary and a donkey would like to be petted. Visit the windmill and the bodega, where you can sample wine and cheese. Old photographs and pottery that was used on the farm are displayed in the farmhouse. Also exhibited in the museum is a collection of beautiful lava stones and rocks. Adjoining the farmhouse are the old winery buildings with a collection of heavy presses and oak barrels.

TINAJO, PLAYA DE TENEZA AND PLAYA DE LA MADERA

Not spectacular, but rather pretty is the long and narrow village of *Tinajo* (127 E2) (𝄞 D7). A good place to eat here is *Mezzaluna (closed Mon | Av. La Cañada 22 | tel. 928840141 | Budget–Moderate)*, where all the Italian classics are served – and that means pizzas from a charcoal oven. Some way from the centre of the village an unmarked road leads to the west coast and the ⚶ *Playa de Teneza* (127 D2) (𝄞 C–D7), then on rough tracks to the *Playa de la Madera* on the edge of Timanfaya National Park (126 C3) (𝄞 B8). The Atlantic waves often break powerfully on both beaches, with the seething waters making an impressive natural spectacle. If you swim here, stay in shallow waters. All too often bathers drown on the west coast, because they underestimate the immense suction power in the retreating sea and are dragged underwater. Now drive towards Caleta de Famara. En route it is worth making the climb to the old ⚶ mill. Stop for a minute and admire the impressive view over the village and the Risco de Famara mountain range.

TIMANFAYA NATIONAL PARK

What a sight! The sea of black lava extends for miles. Towering above it in the distance are mountains, many with decapitated peaks. Others rise gently, but all are covered with granules of lava shimmering in a range of colours from beige and grey to rust-red.

Clouds cast bizarre shadows, the wind scurries across the plain, whistling between jagged chunks of magma, stirring up the tiny lapilli, the lava shingle that lies in layers three feet deep. These droplets of molten or semi-molten lava are known on the Canaries as *picón*. Not a single tree or shrub interrupts the monotony. It's a lunar landscape.

The *Montañas del Fuego*, the Fire Mountains, evoke a degree of trepidation in everyone who visits this desolate region.

One of the worst catastrophes recorded in the history of the modern world happened here. The volcanic eruptions on Lanzarote lasted for six years, from 1730 to 1736. They buried almost a quarter of the island and left behind the largest field of lava in the world. Many lanzaroteños fled to Gran Canaria. Many places were either buried by clouds of ash or devastated by streams of lava that afterwards flowed on into the sea. Millions of fish died, only to wash up later along the coast. New mountains rose, craters were formed and exploded on the same day, chasms opened up. The heat burnt the fields and cattle succumbed to the poisonous vapours.

In 1824 the peace was shattered again. Three more volcanoes were formed but

Photo: Road leading through the Montañas del Fuego in Timanfaya National Park

The place that brought catastrophe to Lanzarote: an inferno still burns beneath the Montañas del Fuego

the devastation bore no comparison to what had happened in the previous century.

Now everything has solidified. The immense power of the volcanic forces can be viewed and admired in safety. The LZ 67 road from Yaiza to Mancha Blanca crosses the forbidding *malpaís*, the "badlands" of solid magma. Rising on the left are the thirty or so cones of the Montañas del Fuego, among them the 510 m (1675-ft) Timanfaya, surrounded by equally impressive companions. The

colours gleam in the sun. The fluorescence is caused by the different minerals in the lava. This collection of conical hills are part of the Timanfaya National Park, a part of which the road crosses. At the *dromedary station*, which you reach at the entrance to the Timanfaya National Park, more than a hundred of these exotic beasts await the arrival of their next passengers. Do stop and take a break here – and a ⭐ ride on a dromedary *(Mon–Fri 9am–3pm | duration approx. 20 minutes | 8 euros per person)* through the peace and stillness of the Timanfaya volcanic mountains. Nearby is a bar, a shop selling souvenirs and a small *museum (Mon–Fri 8am–3pm)* exhibiting lava stones from the national park.

The following ☙ pass affords a magnificent view over the sea of lava. Here the access road to the centre of the National Park forks off. Its symbol, a malevolent-looking demon, El Diablo, welcomes you to his kingdom. It was another product of César Manrique's fertile imagination.

PARQUE NACIONAL DE TIMANFAYA

(126 A–C   3–5) (*𝄞 B–C 8–9*)   **Lunar landscape? Trip to hell? Bowels of the earth? At Timanfaya National Park you will feel as though you have just landed on a different planet. Its name is de-** rived from a village that disappeared under the lava.

From the LZ 67 a narrow asphalt road branches off to a cabin made from dark lava stone. After paying the admission fee continue for another two miles to the *Islote de Hilario,* a vantage point rising from the flat landscape like an islet *(islote).* At its summit are the visitor centre and the ☙ *Restaurante del Diablo (Moderate),* the "Devil's Restaurant" that Manrique built from lava stone and fireproof materials. Panoramic windows with views in all directions surround the circular building. Even if you don't want to eat, look out the glass across the bleak, lava-strewn landscape. On a massive barbecue powered by heat from the centre of the earth, cooks grill steaks, while outside park wardens demonstrate what is happening below the thin crust of lava: Brushwood is thrown into a shallow pit outside the restaurant and ignites spontaneously. When a bucket of water is emptied into a pipe set deep in the earth, the water hisses as it evaporates. At a depth of 10 cm the temperature is 140 °C/284 °F, at 6 m it's 400°C/752 °F. *Daily 9am–5:45pm | admission 9 euros*

LOW BUDGET

● The longer guided walks from the visitor centre near Mancha Blanca are free *(register at least 14 days in advance, exclusively online via www. reservasparquesnacionales.es | from 16 years).* The geology and biology explanations are in Spanish and English; the tours through the jagged lava with eight participants mostly take place on Mon, Wed and Fri.

No charge either to enter the multimedia-oriented, very informative visitor centre.

SIGHTSEEING

RUTA DE LOS VOLCANES ★ ☙
(126 C4) (*𝄞 C9*)
The highlight of the national park is the 45-minute journey along the 14 km (6 miles) volcano route. It is not open to private cars; the only way to explore the park is a bus tour from the Islote de Hilario. The tour goes deep into a surreal world, where it seems as if dozens of meteorites have struck the earth, each forming its own craters. It's a lesson in vulcanology: look out for the steep-sided *hornitos* (small ovens) or 100 m/328 ft

A caravan plods through, but everyone else had better keep out

diameter *calderas*. There are collapsed lava tunnels and huge ash slides. As the bus continues its journey through hell you listen to heroic music by Wagner and Beethoven, as if the landscape wasn't already dramatic enough! You will also hear spoken diary entries by the priest from Yaiza who witnessed the eruptions of 1730 that changed Lanzarote so drastically. The tour is included in the national park admission. **INSIDER TIP** Avoid the overbooked lunchtime hours! *Departures every 30 minutes, last bus 5pm*

INFORMATION & TOURS

VISITOR CENTRE ●
(127 D3–4) (*𝄞 D8*)
The architecturally stunning *Centro de Visitantes e Interpretación de Mancha Blanca (daily 9am–5pm | admission free | on the LZ 67, km 9.6 | tel. 928 84 08 39 | www.tinajo.es/centro_visitantes_tinajo. php)* explains the background to the Fire Mountains using interactive panels, exhibitions, photographs, a film and lava

to touch. It also deals with the culture and the everyday life of the island's inhabitants. A boardwalk takes visitors a long way out onto the inhospitable expanse of black clinker.

For a closer look at the volcanoes, take a guided tour *(see also Low Budget box on p. 74)*, e.g. the *Ruta de Tremesana* (130 C2) (*𝄞 B–C9*) which follows a route along the southern edge of the national park past craters and lava tubes and an almost level lava lake.

★ **Dromedary rides**
A ride through the volcanic ash fields in Timanfaya National Park on the back of a dromedary is an amazing experience → p. 73

★ **Ruta de los Volcanes**
The highlight of any visit to Timanfaya is a tour through the park's lunar landscape → p. 74

MARCO POLO HIGHLIGHTS

PLAYA BLANCA AND THE SOUTH

It's not unlike the Sahara Desert: barren land, parched by the sun, a few scrubby growths of lichen and dried grasses – the desert can have a mesmerising effect.

Although small thorn bushes cling tenaciously to the soil and spiky globes wave in the wind like a scene from a Western film, the pool, the beach and a cooling drink are never far away. Faintly visible in the heat, a settlement of white, low-rise buildings shimmers in the distance. Approach a little closer and it grows into a jumble of villas and hotels: Playa Blanca.

The southern end of the island is by far the driest region of Lanzarote. And that means: sunshine guaranteed! This is also why the fishing village of Playa Blanca became one of the island's three main tourist centres. Outside the mega-resort, you will find the Playas de Papagayo, the most magnificent beaches, as well as the island's most popular nudist beaches.

Opposite lie the island of Fuerteventura and a small offshore island, Isla de Lobos. Shuttle across by ferry or excursion boat or take a pleasure cruise.

PLAYA BLANCA

(130 B5–6) (*M A–B 11–12*) Once there was just a remote fishing village in this barren region, now there's a sprawling

The perfect destination for weather-distressed northern Europeans: sunshine and holiday fun are guaranteed in Lanzarote's hot south

conurbation of whitewashed holiday villages.

The architecture of the villas and hotels is worth a closer look, and luxuriant gardens awash with colourful bougainvillea do wonders for the overall impression of Playa Blanca (pop. 10,000). The extensive resort which is spread out over a flat plain is perfect for families and elderly people. Its plus points are proximity to the fantastic Playas de Papagayo and the almost unbroken sunshine.

The spacious, pedestrianised promenade is the heart of Playa Blanca – here you can take a relaxed stroll while looking out to sea towards the neighbouring islands. At the town beach the atmosphere is family-oriented, and the restaurants and apartments are restricted to a height of two or three storeys. Heading westwards, the promenade continues for miles to the lighthouse, *Faro de Pechiguera*. To the east, it extends from the ferry port as far as the vast *Marina Rubicón* and the *Castillo de las Coloradas*.

Unfortunately, over time, monumental hotels have begun to encroach on the paradise beaches. Row after row of villa and apartment complexes have slowly crept inland onto the parched plain.

MUSEO ATLÁNTICO DE LANZAROTE ★

Have you ever wanted to dive into a museum? Now you can at Europe's first undersea museum: 400 quite realistic, life-sized concrete figures are waiting for you

The yacht harbour Marina Rubicón is a popular place for a stroll both day and night

SIGHTSEEING

CASTILLO DE LAS COLORADAS ☼

Even down here on the south coast, the fishing communities were not immune from pirate attacks, and the villages were repeatedly pillaged. It is said that the conqueror Jean de Béthencourt once built a fortress here. The present castle dates from 1769. Its name derives from the colourful *(coloradas)* rocks along the coast. Unfortunately the massive circular tower is not open to visitors and is now partially blocked off by hotels. It is worth making the trip to the Punta del Águila promontory for fine views along the colourful cliffs as far as the nearby Papagayo beaches, over the Marina Rubicón and, if the weather is fine, to Fuerteventura.

at a depth of 12–15 m/39–49 ft. British artist Jason deCaires Taylor arranged the figures in everyday situations: refugees on the "Raft of Lampedusa", a couple taking a selfie, people crowding in front of a wall... The artist hopes that an artificial reef full of diverse species of fish will someday evolve as aquatic plants take over the sculptures. On calm days when the water is clear, it is possible to look down to the exhibits from a boat. Otherwise, dive or snorkel down! A visit to the museum must be booked through an authorised diving school. But that is not a problem: practically all diving schools on Lanzarote offer the tour, e.g. *Windblue Sports* (see p. 80). *Daily from Marina Rubicón 10am–4pm | admission for divers 12 euros, for* snorkelers 8 euros, plus the obligatory organised dive starting at 30 euros (approx. 2–3 hours) | www.cactlanzarote.com/cact/museo-atlantico

FOOD & DRINK

BAR ONE ●
Whatever the time of day, this is the perfect place to chill out over a snack, while watching the yachts come and go. Inexpensive lunch-time menu. *Daily | Marina Rubicón | tel. 928 34 99 30 | Budget–Moderate*

BODEGÓN LAS TAPAS
Tapas consumed in large quantities in this rustic setting surrounded by wine barrels. Overlooking the promenade and the sea. *Closed Sun | Paseo Marítimo 5 | tel. 928 51 83 10 | Budget–Moderate*

CASA BRÍGIDA ●
One of the island's well-known food experts, Pedro Santana, dons an apron himself in the kitchen of this restaurant serving creative and delicious Canarian cuisine. If you're not sure what to order, try the six-course set menu for 30 euros – you won't be disappointed! *Daily 1pm–11pm | Puerto Marina Rubicón, Local 32 B | tel. 928 51 91 90 | www.restaurante casabrigida.com | Moderate*

LA CASA ROJA
The "red house" with its panoramic windows sits on a wooden pier overlooking the marina crammed with smart yachts. Setting elegant, cuisine upmarket Mediterranean with the emphasis on fish and seafood. Recently, this classic go-to restaurant has met with increased criticism coming from diners. Nonetheless, it is still worth trying the parrotfish paté and the squid carpaccio plus the mojito sorbet as

dessert! *Daily | Marina Rubicón | tel. 928 51 96 44 | www.lacasaroja-lanzarote.com | Moderate*

INSIDER TIP SEBASTYAN'S ☆
Done all in blue and white, this elegant restaurant is situated high above the promenade. From its lofty vantage point you can see all the way to Fuerteventura as you enjoy wonderfully prepared classics of Greek-Mediterranean cuisine. The restaurant also has a wine cellar with a large selection of wines. Be sure to make a reservation for the evening. *Daily | Centro Comercial La Mulata L. 4 | C/ Lanzarote (direction of*

the lighthouse) | tel. 9 28 34 96 79 | www. sebastykans.com | *Moderate*

SHOPPING

Shops line the pedestrian-friendly street Calle Limones.

FUNDACIÓN CÉSAR MANRIQUE
More from the grand master, even here in Playa Blanca. *Av. Papagayo 8*

MERCADILLO
A small market surrounded by the lovely ambiance of the yacht harbour where you can buy local arts and crafts. *Wed and Sat 9am–2pm | Costa Papagayo and Marina Rubicón*

INSIDER TIP ▶ MODA INDIGO
Light fabrics are the stuff of modern fashion – at least on Lanzarote. Locally-based designers, such as Romy B, design casual collections and accessories in high-quality linen. *C/ Limones 56 | www.romyb.info*

LOW BUDGET

Los Hervideros (closed Tue | C/ El Marisco 9 | tel. 928 517 707), a family-run restaurant, is the cheapest in Playa Blanca; low-budget lunchtime menus.

Tourist passes to Lanzarote's tourist attractions are sold at all information centres. The *bonos* are valid for 14 days and usually cost less than it would to buy the individual tickets. Passes for six attractions *(Timanfaya, Jardín de Cactus, Jameos del Agua, Cueva de los Verdes, Mirador del Río, Castillo de San José)* cost 30 euros, four 26 eurosand three20 euros.

MYSTIC
Pamper yourself, but with natural materials: sponges, brushes and beach towels. *Av. Marítima*

BEACHES

There are three fine bathing beaches in the resort itself: there's the small, sandy beach beneath the promenade near the town centre; to the west, beneath the Lanzarote Park hotel, the *Playa Flamingo* and finally east of the town beach the *Playa Dorada.* The two last-named beaches have fine, golden sand and also loungers and parasols for hire. Breakwaters ensure totally safe bathing in clear water. The neigbouring *Playas de Papagayo (see p. 85)* are even nicer.

LEISURE & SPORTS

Kayak tours, SUP and snorkelling sessions are offered by *Windblue Sports (C/ Los Bebederos 20 | tel. 9 28 51 96 06 | www.windbluesports.com)*; they also run a scuba diving base *(www.windbluediving.com)*. You can also hire a pedalo *(6 euros per person | on the Playa Dorada)* or have fun in a speedboat or a banana boat *(in the harbour at Playa Blanca).* Excursions in local waters leave from here. A number of boat operators run trips to the Papagayo beaches and the Isla de los Lobos. A free bus takes guests to Puerto Calero for expeditions in a submarine *(from 46,75 euros | www.submarinesafaris.com).* You can also swim at the *Aqualava Waterpark (see p. 107)* – especially the kids like it.

All four- and five-star hotels in Playa Blanca have modern spa facilities. The town's no. 1 spa is at the *Hotel Princesa Yaiza (Av. Papagayo 22 | www.princesayaiza.com),* where the health and

Shorts have already been crossed off the shopping list: market stalls on the promenade

beauty team use ingredients sourced on the island. The emphasis is on treatments that follow the correct medical and cosmetic guidelines. All therapists are professionally trained and multilingual.

ENTERTAINMENT

It's fun to sit and drink a glass of wine or a beer on the promenade and follow it with a cocktail in the marina. Just a few steps away, you can listen to live music ranging from flamenco to funk every evening after 8pm at the *Blue Note Club* (www.bluenotelanzarote.com). From Thursday to Saturday evening, it's worthwile to go to the stylish *Jazz Club Cuatro Lunas* in the Hotel Princesa Yaiza. Expect to hear top-class live music or themed partys from "Halloween" to "Fiesta Cubana".

On the other side of the town centre, towards the Faro de Pechiguera, the ● *Marea Lounge Club* (daily until 3:30am) provides a green terrace on the promenade, the ideal place to chill out and watch the sun set over Fuerteventura. Live music afterwards.

WHERE TO STAY

GRAN CASTILLO TAGORO ✹
All-inclusive five-star hotel built in typical Andalusian style around a Spanish fantasy castle, situated by the sea near the Papagayo beaches. Spacious, attractive rooms, large pool area, view of Fuerteventura, spa, kid's club and nightly entertainment in the "theatre". Guests sing the praises of the breakfast and evening buffets that are also served outside. *279 rooms | Urbanización Las Coloradas | tel. 928 59 59 99 | www.dreamplacehotels.com | Expensive*

THE HOTEL VOLCÁN LANZAROTE
The entrance to this five-star hotel passes through a "church", which is an exact replica of the one in Teguise, before entering a life-size "volcano". A Canarian village with Mediterranean-inspired houses as well as lagoon-like pools are built around it. Another plus

point is the INSIDER TIP luxurious club area offering an intimate atmosphere and lots of inclusive extras such as coffee & cake as well evening cocktails. The hotel also has a lovely spa, a gym, free tennis and paddles, workshops and a kid's club. *255 rooms | C/ El Castillo 1 | Urbanización Castillo del Águila | tel. 9 28 51 91 85 | www.hotelvolcanolanzarote.com | Expensive*

INFORMATION

C/ Limones 1 (tel. 928 518150 | www.ayuntamientodeyaiza.es); there's another information pavilion by the marina.

WHERE TO GO

EL GOLFO AND CHARCO DE LOS CLICOS ⠴ (130 B2–3) (𝔐 A9)

Like the Fire Mountains, the deep green ★ *Charco de los Clicos lagoon (admis-*

White wine or red wine with the cheese? But why not keep switching between the two?

IBEROSTAR LANZAROTE PARK ⠴

The hotel is perched on a cape jutting into the sea, only a few steps from Flamingo beach. Studios in maritime colours with kitchenette and sea view balcony; rooms on the ground floor with direct access to the pool gardens are ideal for families. Good buffets, "dine around", i.e. if you book half-board you can also eat in the sister Papagayo Hotel. *Urbanización Montaña Roja | tel. 928 51 70 48 | www.iberostar.com | Moderate*

sion fee planned) has also featured in a science-fiction movie. Shaped like a sickle, the lake fills a sunken volcanic crater, half of which is in a cove by the sea. The walls of the crater have been eroded by wind. What makes this lake such an attraction is the unusual colour of the water. Sea water, which after evaporation has a higher salt content, remains trapped in the crater and, due to special algae, then turns a bright green. The contrast with the tar-black lava sand, the dark blue Atlantic and the white spray is striking. Access on foot: from the car-park by the country lane to the south of the lagoon and from the car-park on the left at the edge of the village of El Golfo.

The country lane ends on the other side of the lagoon in the fishing village of *El Golfo*. It's perhaps hard to believe, but the entire village, together with hotel and restaurants, is threatened with demolition. According to Spanish law, houses less than 100 m/328 ft from the sea at low tide are illegal. As houses in similar coastal locations elsewhere in the Canaries have been summarily torn down, the inhabitants of El Golfo fear the worst.

Despite the threat hanging over the village, it can still boast some of the best fish restaurants in Lanzarote. You eat on beautiful terraces by the sea. The best restaurants: *Lago Verde (closed Tue | Av. Marítima 46 | tel. 928 17 33 11 | Moderate–Expensive)* and *Bogavante (daily | Av. Marítima 39 | tel. 928 17 35 05 | Moderate–Expensive).*

For the best value for your money, head to INSIDER TIP *Casa Rafa (closed Mon | Av. Marítima | tel. 6 25 10 43 30 | www.restaurantedemar.com | Moderate)* with its small menu but large portions and good house wines! Make sure to try the desserts: INSIDER TIP homemade ice cream in unusual flavours as well as the spongy, creamy cheesecake *(tarta de queso).*

El Hotelito (Av. Marítima 6 | tel. 928 17 32 72 | hotelitodelgolfo.com | Budget) is a lovely place to stay. This "miniature hotel" has only nine rooms, some with a sea view. The proprietor, Isabel, will ensure you get personal service. This hotel is a refuge for independent travellers looking for total peace and tranquillity.

FARO DE PECHIGUERA ☙
(130 A6) (*ℳ A12*)

There is a good road to the lighthouse, which lies 3 km (2 miles) west of Playa Blanca, but the pleasant walk to this conspicuous landmark only takes about an hour. The path follows the coastline, passing the attractive Playa Flamingo as well as the new hotels and apartment complexes on the shoreline. Built in 1986, the lighthouse is not in itself particularly impressive, but the view over to Fuerteventura is wonderful.

FEMÉS ★ ☙
(130 C4) (*ℳ B10–11*)

The name, *Balcón de Femés,* is fully justified. If the weather is fine, from this pass at 450 m (1475 ft) you get an amazing view over the Rubicón plain, far beyond Playa Blanca and across to Isla de Lobos and Fuerteventura.

Femés is not much more than a cluster of houses, but the village can boast three decent restaurants. Eat in the ☙ *Balcón de Femés (daily | tel. 928 11 36 18 | Moderate)* directly at the viewing platform. The *Casa Emiliano (closed Mon | tel. 928 83 02 23 | Moderate),* on the other hand, is a set back a little, but has superb food and a pretty terrace. The *Restaurante Femés (daily | no phone | Budget)* is on the plaza. There is no view, but the locals eat here. Try the goat's cheese from Femés. Before you decide which kind to choose, you can try free samples at the small *Quesería de Rubicón (Mon–Sat 10am–8pm, Sun 10am–3pm | Plaza de San Marcial 3)* in the shadow of the church with a sip of wine from their own bodega.

FUERTEVENTURA (0) (*ℳ A14*)

You can see Lanzarote's big sister from anywhere on Playa Blanca. Would you like to meet her? It only takes 30 min-

Where nature presents itself most dramatically: Los Hervideros

utes for the ferry to cross from Playa Blanca to the harbour at Corralejo on the neighbouring island. It leaves on the hour from 7am and the last return crossing is scheduled for 8pm. In the "Discovery Tours" chapter, you'll find a detailed description of a detour to Fuerteventura; more detailed information in the MARCO POLO guide "Fuerteventura".

LOS HERVIDEROS ⭐
(130 B3) (*📖 A10*)

The water bubbles and hisses at Los Hervideros ("the boiling waters"), which lie between the Salinas de Janubio and El Golfo. This impressive spectacle of caves, chimneys and arches has occurred through tidal erosion of the porous lava rock. At high tide, and especially when the Atlantic is rough and heavy swells roll in, the water crashes through them and up into the air with great force. A set of angled paths and staircases lead to a viewing platform amidst the melee. A surfaced car-park is located at the side.

MONTAÑA ROJA 🌿
(130 A–B 5–6) (*📖 A11*)

If visitors to Playa Blanca need some exercise after too much lounging around on the beach, it's not far to Montaña Roja. It is an easy, quick climb (but without any shade!) to the top of the Red Mountain (194 m/636 ft), the nearest volcano to Playa Blanca, and the only elevation on the southern El Rubicón plain. The ascent starts above the Montaña Baja holiday complex along a well-worn, easily visible footpath and it takes not much longer than half an hour. At the top there is an equally good footpath around the entire crater. The view from up here encompasses Playa Blanca and the Papagayo beaches, to the south Fuerteventura is usually clearly visible. Further west, endless apartment blocks, some only half-finished, spoil the panoramic view.

PLAYAS DE PAPAGAYO ★
(130 C6) (*B12*)

The beaches some 3.2 to 5.5 km (2 to 3.5 miles) east of Playa Blanca are renowned for their beauty. Framed by rocks, the beaches here are covered with fine, golden sand; the turquoise water is beautifully clean. In addition, the currents are usually weak and the waves gentle, so that children can safely swim and paddle.

The beaches are only accessible by car via a signposted track (*3 euros*). The admission charge also includes entry to the nature reserve, the *Monumento Natural de los Ajaches*, to which the beaches belong. Large car-parks are to be found near the Playa Mujeres, above the Playa Papagayo and by the wilder Playa Caleta del Congrio. The Papagayo beaches can easily be reached INSIDERTIP in only 15 minutes on foot from the district of Las Coloradas. Park on the road in front of the Papagayo Arena Hotel and follow the signposted footpath to the south. This way you avoid the rough track and save 3 euros.

All beaches are easy to access, even the highly recommended smaller ones: Playa del Pozo, Playa de la Cera and Playa

de Puerto Muelas. When the tide is out, you can walk from one beach to the next.

SALINAS DE JANUBIO ★ ●
(130 B3–4) (*A–B10*)

Forming long rows of rectangular fields in varying sizes in iridescent browns, reds, greys and blacks and resembling a giant patchwork quilt, the Saline de Janubio is situated below the road to Playa Blanca. Sea salt used to be of vital importance for the fishing community, as it was needed to conserve the precious catch – and their own provisions. Wind pumps, which have fallen into disrepair, pumped the seawater up 40 m/130 ft into the largest basins. From there it was gradually discharged into the smallest basins, after undergoing a series of ingenious evaporation stages. The workers then collected the crystallised salt into mounds using wooden rakes.

During the 19th century, the salt pans still yielded more than 10,000 tons of salt every year. Only small quantities are harvested now. You can buy this ◐ tasty coarse sea salt on the edge of the salt fields at *Bodega de Janubio (Mon–Fri 9am–2pm | LZ 703, km 2 | www.salinasdejanubio.com)*. Unlike industrial salt which is produced in large vacuum evaporation plants, sea salt is a purely natu-

BORN IN HELL

You often find them on the black lava beaches on the west coast: small, green, shimmering pebbles of ● olivine. The mineral was hurled upwards from the bowels of the earth together with the magma and later washed out of the clinker by the sea. Pieces of lava studded with olivine are sold as

souvenirs, e.g. at Los Hervideros and El Golfo, for 1 to 3 euros. Many other shops sell jewellery using this pretty semi-precious stone. However, most of it comes not from the island but from South America and Asia, as the fragments found on Lanzarote are usually too small.

ral product harvested manually. It is rich in calcium, magnesium and iodine. From the ☀ *Mirador Las Salinas Casa Domingo* restaurant *(daily 11am–9pm | C/ Hervidero 7 | tel. 9 28 17 30 70 | Moderate)* you have an extensive view over the salt pans. INSIDER TIP The colours are beautiful at sunset! The food is excellent as well – how about *pescado a la sal,* fish baked gently in a salt crust? Walk over the lava beach below the saltworks if you want to take a closer look at the salts.

UGA (130 D3) (*∅ C10*)

This tiny, oasis-like village with dazzling white, cuboid houses, palm trees and an African-sounding name is also home to the dromedaries, which trek across the Fire Mountains bearing daytrippers. When their day's work is done, they are usually to be seen passing the Uga–Yaiza roundabout (where a giant monument was erected in their honour) between 4:30pm and 5pm. Uga is also well known for its *salmon smokehouse* situated on the road to Arrecife (but beware: the minimum purchase is 500 g!).

Casa Gregorio in the village *(closed Tue | tel. 928 83 01 08 | Budget–Moderate)* is highly regarded for its inexpensive and delicious Lanzarotean fare.

YAIZA (130–131 C–D3) (*∅ B–C10*)

This is what César Manrique wanted to see throughout the island: gleaming white houses, bright green window shutters and flowering geraniums. Yaiza is Lanzarote's model village and has already won several "beauty competitions". One particularly harmonious ensemble is to be found around the 17th-century church of *Nuestra Señora de los Remedios* and the two adjoining squares. It is worth taking a look inside the church with its exposed bells in the bell tower: the Madonna statue on the high altar is bathed in a mysterious blue light shining in through the church windows. Every year on 8 September, the figure leads a procession through the village. Opposite the church is the low white *Casa de la Cultura (Mon–Fri 9am–1pm and 5pm–7pm)*, Yaiza's cultural centre. Built in the 19th century, it was from 1871 to 1937 the

MOVIE SET LANZAROTE

"I have never seen so many dramatic colours in nature – so dark and so bright," Spain's star director Pedro Almodóvar effusively described Lanzarote. No wonder that he filmed "Broken Embraces" (2009) here and also bought a villa in Puerto Calero. Lanzarote's landscapes have often served as a bizarre setting for films – particularly for fantasy and science fiction films. Few remember director Don Chaffey, but thanks to Raquel Welch, his Stone Age thriller "One Million Years B.C." (1966) has

achieved cult status: the actress photogenically skipped through the Fire Mountains in a fur bikini. In Wolfgang Petersen's "Enemy Mine" (1985), humans and gods faced off in the labyrinth of caves called Cueva de los Verdes. The Fire Mountains also provided the setting for the fantasy remake "Clash of the Titans" (2010). These will not be the last, of course: filmmakers gather here every year for the film festival *(www.festivaldecinedelanzarote. com)*.

And they look good, too: the salt pans of the Salinas de Janubio

residence of the Spanish politician and writer, Benito Pérez Armas, and is now used for temporary exhibitions. Artworks are also displayed in the INSIDER TIP Galería Yaiza (Mon–Sat 5–7pm | Ctra. General 13/LZ-2), the beautifully restored former village smithy – Lanzarote's erfirst private gallery (1984): Expressive paintings, virtuosic drawings and etchings at affordable prices! The former school, the Antigua Escuela (C/ La Cuesta 1/LZ 2) at the opposite end of the village is also worth seeking out. Instead of classrooms, it houses a bistro-café and interesting shops selling jewellery and handicrafts. The range of goods in La Route des Caravanes is a scene from the Arabian Nights. An evocative place to spend the night is the INSIDER TIP Casona de Yaiza (C/ El Rincón 11 | tel. 928 83 62 62 | www.ca sonadeyaiza.com | Moderate) with eight suites grouped around a courtyard as well as a cosy bodega. The real charm of this hotel lies in the underground cisterns that have been turned into luxurious parlours.

Another good choice is the ● Casa de Hilario (7 rooms | Ctra. García Escámez 19 | tel. 928 83 62 62 | www.casadehilario. com| Expensive). The view from the pool terrace takes in the sea and the forbidding outline of the Fire Mountains. The rooms and lounges, eccentrically decorated with chinoiserie, hark back to a bygone era. INSIDER TIP La Bodega Santiago (closed Mon | LZ 67 | on the road to the Fire Mountains | tel. 9 28 83 62 04 | Moderate), a quaint country inn, is located right next door. Lanzarote wines accompany creative twists on Canarian cuisine – tuna carpaccio with marinated sea snails, langoustine salad with mini beans and the best fillet of beef. Ask Juan Carlos about his daily specials!

DISCOVERY TOURS

① LANZAROTE AT A GLANCE

START: ① Playa Blanca **END:** ① Playa Blanca	3 days Driving time (without stops) 6.5 hours
Distance: 🚗 200 km/124 miles	

COSTS: accommodation approx. 150 euros, restaurant meal 15–25 euros/person

WHAT TO PACK: sun protection, swim gear

IMPORTANT TIPS: As the distances on Lanzarote are quite manageable, it is not necessary to stay in the hotels mentioned below. You can easily stop the tour at any point and return to your pre-booked accommodation for the night!

If you plan to visit several of the landscape artworks of César Manrique, you can save money by purchasing a voucher valid for multiple sites *(bono, see p. 80).*

Would you like to explore the places that are unique to this island? Then the Discovery Tours are just the thing for you – they include terrific tips for stops worth making, breathtaking places to visit, selected restaurants and fun activities. It's even easier with the Touring App: download the tour with map and route to your smartphone using the QR Code on pages 2/3 or from the website address in the footer below – and you'll never get lost again even when you're offline.

TOURING APP

→ p. 2/3

A tour of contrasts! Experience black fire mountains, green valleys moistened by trade winds, coastal villages and colonial Teguise. Along the way, discover the most beautiful works of landscape art on Lanzarote ranging from viewing platforms, underground cave worlds and unusual gardens fit for a real desert to emerald green lagoons and glistening salt fields.

Get an early start so you have enough time – 9am is perfect! **From ① Playa Blanca** → p. 76**, take the LZ 702 towards the island's interior. You will first cross a dusty plateau, then the road climbs steeply up to the village**

DAY 1

① Playa Blanca

8 km/5 mi

Photo: Playas de Papagayo

Lanzarote

Parque Natural del Archipielago Chinijo

Montaña Clara 256
Graciosa
Caleta del Sebo 266
Pedro Barba
Caleta del Sebo
Río
Orzola
El Río
Jameos del Agua
Cueva de los Verdes
La Bahía de Penedo
Haría
Pta. Prieta
La Isleta
La Santa
Caleta de Famara
Peñas del Chache 671
Tabayesco
Pta. Gaviota
Sóo
Mala
Guatiza
Parque Nac. de Timanfaya
Tinajo
Teguise
Los Cocoteros
Mancha Blanca
Tiagua
550 20
Castillo de Guanapay
Islote de Hilario
Masdache
San Bartolomé
Pta. de Tierra Negra
Fuego 510
Güime
San José
El Golfo
Castillo de S. Gabriel
Tías
Mácher
Arrecife
Yaiza
Pta. de la Lagarta
Las Breñas
Femés 608
Femés
Playa Quemada
Puerto del Carmen
Las Coloradas
Playa Blanca
Playa de Papagayo
Punta del Papagayo

Estrecho de La Bocaina

10 km
6.21 mi

2 Femés
8 km/5 mi

3 Yaiza
6 km/3.75 mi

4 Montañas del Fuego
200 m/219 yd

5 Parque Nacional de Timanfaya

of **2 Femés** → p. 83, located on the eroded slope of the Ajaches massif. From the viewing platform, you can trace the way you came and see the neighbouring island of Fuerteventura on the horizon. **From Femés, follow the road through the upper valley to the Yaiza-Arrecife road. Head left to get to the picturesque village of 3 Yaiza** → p. 86, which shines like a beacon of white-green against the dark landscape – an ideal place for a short walk.

Then take the LZ 67 towards the 4 Montañas del Fuego → p. 72, the "Fire Mountains" in the **5 Parque Nacional de Timanfaya** → p. 74. INSIDER TIP It pays to come early in order to avoid the crowds so that you can enjoy the magnificent landscape without feeling rushed. The start of the lava fields is marked by wooden signs on which a small devil, the *Diablo de Timanfaya*, sits as if on a throne. Shortly thereafter, you will come to the **⑥ Dromedary station → p. 73**. Don't be afraid to take a ride on these Arabian camels because you're sure to enjoy it. **Afterwards, you will come to a fork in the road leading to ⑦ Islote de Hilario → p. 74**, which will bring you to the "heart" of the national park. On the round-trip bus tour, you will get to see the most spectacular places in the Fire Mountains – there are black lava flows, cones and craters everywhere you look! Then you can grab a bite to eat for lunch at the circular **⑧ Restaurante del Diablo → p. 74** as you enjoy the views of the Fire Mountains. At the **⑨ Centro de Visitantes e Interpretación de Mancha Blanca → p. 75**, you can learn all about the mysterious volcanic world around you.

You can also explore what life was like on the farms here in days past at the **⑩ Museo Agrícola El Patio → p. 71**. **Located in Tiagua to the northeast of the national park,** this lovingly furnished old farmstead is nestled within a sub-tropical garden. The **⑪ Monumento al Campesino → p. 68 – southwards on the LZ 20 –** pays homage to the farmers on the island. You can also buy traditional arts and crafts right next door. The hotel **⑫ Caserío de Mozaga → p. 69** offers lovely rooms for the night.

On the next day, take the LZ 30 straight to ⑬ Teguise → p. 52. The old capital with its white houses, monasteries and churches is the most historically significant town on the island. Stroll through this treasure trove of colonial architecture that bustles with business on Sundays when it plays host to a large market – expect crowds and full car parks on these days. Then you can really look forward to capturing the magnificent views at the **⑭ Ermita de las Nieves → p. 56**. This chapel near the highest peak on the island offers an impressive view of the west coast of Lanzarote. **Now it is time to head down deep into the valley of 1,000 palm trees that turns into an oasis when it rains.** Nestled in the middle of the valley, you will find the pretty village of **⑮ Haría → p. 56** with its quiet streets and squares. You should have no trouble finding a place to park unless you visit during the little market held on Sundays – then it's best to park outside the centre. **After Haría, the LZ 201 climbs back up** to the point where it looks like the edge of Lanzarote was cut with an axe, dropping into

200 m/219 yd

⑥ Dromedary station

5 km/3 mi

⑦ Islote de Hilario

5 km/3 mi

⑧ Restaurante del Diablo

5 km/3 mi

⑨ Centro de Visitantes e Interpretación de Mancha Blanca

10 km/6.2 mi

⑩ Museo Agrícola El Patio

6 km/3.75 mi

⑪ Monumento al Campesino

700 m/766 yd

⑫ Caserío de Mozaga

DAY 2

8 km/5 mi

⑬ Teguise

11 km/6.8 mi

⑭ Ermita de las Nieves

8 km/5 mi

⑮ Haría

9 km/5.6 mi

⑯ Mirador del Río ☀

10 km/6.2 mi

⑰ Órzola 🍴

9 km/5.6 mi

⑱ Jameos del Agua

1 km/0.6 mi

⑲ Cueva de los Verdes ☀🎵

5 km/3 mi

⑳ Arrieta 🏃

8 km/5 mi

㉑ Jardín de Cactus 🌵

12 km/7.5 mi

㉒ Fundación César Manrique 🏛

6 km/3.75 mi

㉓ Arrecife 🛏🏨

DAY 3

25 km/15.5 mi

㉔ La Geria 🏠🍷

4 km/2.5 mi

the sea. Enjoy the breathtaking views from the panoramic windows of the ⑯ **Mirador del Río** → p. 58 across the strait between Lanzarote and the island of La Graciosa. Fill up on some tasty seafood at one of the restaurants in the fishing village of ⑰ **Órzola** → p. 48. **The route along the LZ 1 to the south will now become quite exciting** as you pass through a hole in the volcanic cover into the ⑱ **Jameos del Agua** → p. 47, which is a system of tunnels that César Manrique transformed into a magical work of art. This underground world is also home to the ⑲ **Cueva de los Verdes** → p. 45. On the 45-minute tour through the multicoloured cave labyrinth, you will hear the music of the spheres – and experience at least one surprise! **Afterwards, continue on the LZ 1 to** ⑳ **Arrieta** → p. 45, which is a good place to take a break on the small promenade. It is also worth stopping in Guatiza at the oversized **metal cactus** that points the way to Manrique's ㉑ **Jardín de Cactus** → p. 47. Thousands of these prickly plants have been artfully arranged in these gardens. Don't miss the former residence of the "great master" in the next village that is now home to the ㉒ **Fundación César Manrique** → p. 46, a fantastic museum built partly within volcanic bubbles. The capital of ㉓ **Arrecife** → p. 32 then awaits with its endearing promenade along the coast. You can find accommodation for the night to fit any budget. A good mid-range hotel is the **Miramar** → p. 39, which offers sea views.

The next morning, take a walk to **El Charco de San Ginés** → p. 35, the town's pretty lagoon. **Afterwards, drive back into the interior of the island. The route through the valley of** ㉔ **La Geria** → p. 68 is unforgettable. It is covered with thousands of recesses in which grapes ripen before

Harvesting grapes the Lanzarote way at the bizarre vineyards in La Geria

they are turned into the wine that you can taste and buy in the bodegas. Pass through **Uga → p. 86** with its seemingly North African charm **to access the LZ 704 to ㉕ El Golfo → p. 83**, which is home to a number of fish restaurants. Take a seat next to the sea and enjoy the fresh fish – an unbeatable ambiance at sunset! If it is not too late, **drive to ㉖ Charco de los Clicos → p. 82**, whose emerald green colour almost seems to be out of this world. End the day with two more highlights, namely ㉗ **Los Hervideros → p. 84**, where the sea swirls through the rocks, and the fascinating geometric saline pools, the ㉘ **Salinas de Janubio → p. 85**. **Then take the LZ 701 back to ❶ Playa Blanca.**

㉕ El Golfo

700 m/766 yd

㉖ Charco de los Clicos

4 km/2.5 mi

㉗ Los Hervideros

4 km/2.5 mi

㉘ Salinas de Janubio

12 km/7.5 mi

❶ Playa Blanca

② DESERT LANDSCAPES AND MONASTERIES: CYCLING AROUND EL JABLE

START: ❶ Costa Teguise **END:** ❶ Costa Teguise	1 day Cycling time (without stops) 4–5 hours

Distance: medium difficulty 🚲 78 km/48 miles ▯▮ Height: 400 m/1,312 ft	

COSTS: admission fees plus bike rental approx. 35 euros
WHAT TO PACK: sun protection, plenty to drink, swim gear

IMPORTANT TIPS: Costa Teguise has several bike hire stations. Start early to take advantage of the cooler morning temperatures. Resume the tour in the afternoon after a swim at La Caleta de Famara.

This tour leads from Costa Teguise to the former capital of Teguise and once around the 40 km² (15.4 miles²) desert of El Jable whose sand is made of finely ground corals, sea shells and snail shells. Blown by the trade winds towards the centre of the island, this glistening white "sand" accumulates on a broad plain at the foot of the Famara massif.

09:00am Starting from ❶ **Costa Teguise → p. 42, go past the greens of the golf course to Tahiche.** The large wind chime at the roundabout tells you that you are getting close to ② **Fundación César Manrique → p. 46**, which gives you a good impression of the artworks of this famous Lanzaroteño. A second residence inspired by him is the fortress-like estate ❸ **Lagomar → p. 58, which you can access via the slightly uphill LZ 10.** After another 2 km (1.2 miles), you will reach ❹ **Teguise → p. 52.** Take your time

❶ Costa Teguise

5 km/3 mi

② Fundación César Manrique

6 km/3.75 mi

❸ Lagomar

3 km/1.9 mi

❹ Teguise

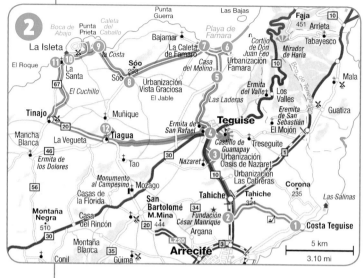

exploring its cobblestone streets and squares. If you are up for a real fitness challenge, then bike up to the **Castillo Santa Bárbara** → p. 53 (an extra 150 m (492 ft) climb!), which is home to a **Pirate Museum**. **Leave Teguise by heading north on the side road and you will soon see the sandy plain of** ⑤ **El Jable** ahead – enjoy the fantastic vista stretching to the bay of Famara and the cliffs above it. At the **Urbanización Famara, you will approach the coast.** The sickle-shaped bungalows looking out to the sea that were built by Norwegians in the 1970s are casually referred to as "goat pens". On the other side of them, you will find the ⑥ **Playa de Famara** → p. 59, which is one of the most beautiful beaches on the Canary Islands thanks to its wild seascape at the foot of tall cliffs! Surfers ride the high swells here, but if you want to head into the water yourself, be careful because there is a dangerous undertow! The best thing to do is to stick close to the shore... **The beach stretches for 4 km (2.5 miles) to the fishing village** ⑦ **La Caleta de Famara**, which still has a seemingly authentic feel with its sand-brushed roads. **After stopping for something to eat, you will bike slightly uphill to the sleepy hamlet of** ⑧. Then the road sinks back down to ⑨ **Caleta de Caballo**. The improvised weekend huts at the sea here do not really fit in with Lanzarote's more stylish image. **Then you will pass by the mega sports hotel La**

10 km/6.2 mi

⑤ El Jable

4 km/2.5 mi

⑥ Playa de Famara

6 km/3.75 mi

⑦ La Caleta de Famara

6 km/3.75 mi

⑧ Sóo

3 km/1.9 mi

⑨ Caleta de Caballo

2 km/1.2 mi

Santa → p. 71. In the winter, many racing cyclists take up residence in this hotel situated on a flat lagoon. The terrace restaurants in the town of ⑩ **La Santa** cater well to the needs of these athletes, offering INSIDERTIP freshly-pressed juices and snacks. Although a little more pricey, Lucy serves up a particularly good meal at ⑪ **Amendôa** *(daily, on Mon evenings only | Av. el Marinero 20 | tel. 9 28 83 82 52 | Moderate)*.

04:00pm In Tinajo, turn onto the LZ 20 to Tiagua. Stop and visit the agricultural museum ⑫ **Museo Agrícola El Patio → p. 71.** Afterwards, follow the LZ 20 for a little bit before turning down a dirt road that runs along the edge of El Jable to Teguise and then follow the way you came through Tahiche back to ① **Costa Teguise.**

⑩ La Santa

⑪ Amendôa

5 km/3 mi

⑫ Museo Agrícola El Patio

20 km/12.4 mi

① Costa Teguise

③ A HIKE THROUGH SEAS OF LAVA

START: ① km 8 on the LZ 67	1 day
END: ① km 8 on the LZ 67	Walking time
Distance: medium difficulty	(without stops)
🚶 8 km/5 miles 📊 Height: 300 m/984 ft	4 hours

WHAT TO PACK: sun protection, sturdy shoes, plenty of water

IMPORTANT TIPS: The trail is easy to follow and well-marked in yellow; the ascent is sometimes steep and demanding. Please bear in mind that you hike at your own risk here.

You can experience the volcanic landscape close-up on foot, but hiking on your own is generally prohibited in the national park. But, you can hike this route that leads up to the impressive Caldera Blanca, crowned with amazing vistas, without a guide.

08:00am **From Mancha Blanca → p. 68, follow the road to Yaiza → p. 86.** When you get to ① **km 8 on the LZ 67**, you will see the start of a lava piste – a sign marks the beginning of the hiking trail. Park your car about 700 m/2,300 ft away – at the end of the piste, which you can easily recognise thanks to the three big lava rocks **at the start of the trail** ② **PR-LZ-19.** The further path of the trail can be seen diagonally to the right – marked by a red arrow as well as a cairn. For about 40 minutes, the trail follows a black lava flow. **After about two-thirds of this stretch of the trail**, look on the right for the hard to find,

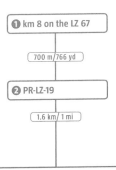

① km 8 on the LZ 67

700 m/766 yd

② PR-LZ-19

1.6 km/1 mi

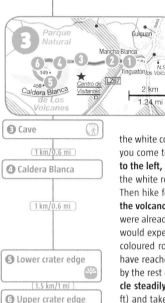

❸ Cave

(1 km/0.6 mi)

❹ Caldera Blanca

(1 km/0.6 mi)

---

❺ Lower crater edge

(1.5 km/1 mi)

❻ Upper crater edge

(5 km/ 3mi)

---

❶ km 8 on the LZ 67

but very pretty ❸ cave with particularly long lava stalactites.

The red volcanic cone provides you with a visual orientation point for the first leg of the hike. **At the foot of this cone and along a wall, you will walk about 10 minutes to the right and then another ten minutes through a lava field.** Keep the white cone of your next stop in view at all times. Once you come to the foot of the ❹ Caldera Blanca, **climb up to the left,** and make sure to stay on the border between the white rocks and the dark lava (approx. ten minutes). Then hike for about another ten minutes **to the right up the volcano;** make sure to stay along the trough that you were already able to discern beforehand. Unlike what you would expect, this fiery mountain is made of hard, light-coloured rocks covered with grey-white spots. Once you have reached the ❺ lower crater edge, don't be fooled by the rest of the ascent – **the trail over the left semi-circle steadily climbs an additional height** of 200 m (656 ft) and takes at least 40 minutes. At the ❻ upper crater edge, at a height of 458 m (1,500 ft), magnificent vistas await on clear days.

`01:00pm` The descent leads to the right over the steeper flank **of the crater a**nd then you follow the same trail back to your car and the starting point of the hike at ❶ return km 8 on the LZ 6

Hiking to Caldera Blanca in a seemingly Martian landscape

MEET THE NEIGHBOURS: HEAD TO FUERTEVENTURA!

START: ❶ Playa Blanca END: ❶ Playa Blanca	1 day Driving time (without stops) 4 hours; ferry 1 hour return
Distance: 🚗 270 km/168 miles	

COSTS: ferry from 27 euros/pers. return (cheapest option: Lineas Romero), rental car from 30 euros, petril approx. 30 euros, restaurant 15–25 euros/pers.

WHAT TO PACK: sun protection, drinks, swim gear

IMPORTANT TIPS: Ferries leave almost every hour between 8am and 7pm from Playa Blanca to Corralejo in the north of Fuerteventura: Naviera Armas *(tel. 9 02 45 65 00 | www.navieraarmas.com)*; Fred Olsen *(tel. 9 02 10 01 07 | www.fredolsen.es)*; Líneas Romero *(tel. 9 28 84 20 55 | www.lineasromero.com)*. Don't forget your ID (also for children!) It's better to rent your car on Fuerteventura, from Cabrera Medina/Cicar *(tel. 9 28 82 29 00 | www.cicar.com)* at Corralejo harbour.

Fuerteventura is home to the loveliest beaches on the Canary Islands as well as an amazing air of solitude that fills the breadth of this old volcanic island. Instead of the dark colours of the Fire Mountains on Lanzarote, you will find tranquil ochre and brown tones and a touch of the wild west rather than stylish villages.

`07:30am` Half an hour after you depart ❶ Playa Blanca → p. 76 with the ferry, you will see the shimmering dunes and attractive seaside promenade as you approach the harbour of **Corralejo** – but you should postpone `INSIDER TIP` a walk through the town until the evening. That way you can spend as much time as you would like before you return to Lanzarote. **From Corralejo, take the FV-101 to the south** through the desolate, sun-drenched landscape and turn right after 5 km/3.1 miles on the FV-109, direction Lajares. It pays to make your first stop in ❷ **El Cotillo**, a friendly fishing village with two small harbours and an old castle. The next stop is the little parish town of ❸ **La Oliva** with some 18th century buildings, including the Candlemas Church and the former colonel's residence **Casa de los Coroneles** *(Tue–Sun 10am–6pm | admission 3 euros | C/ Juan Cabrera Méndez)* with an art gallery arranged around a palm

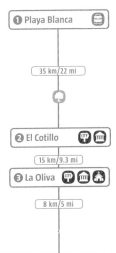

❶ Playa Blanca

35 km / 22 mi

❷ El Cotillo

15 km / 9.3 mi

❸ La Oliva

8 km / 5 mi

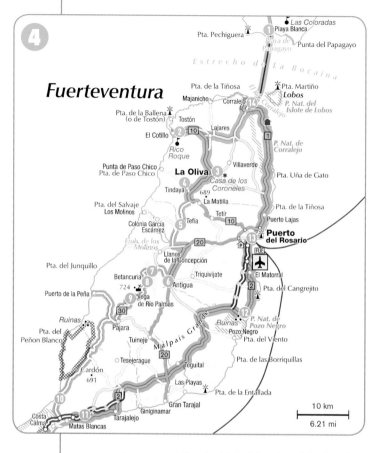

Fuerteventura

tree courtyard. You should also take a look at the Canarian art displayed in the neighbouring **Casa Mané** (Mon–Fri 10am–5pm, Sat 10am–2pm | admission 4 euros | C/ Salvador Manrique de Lara). **Then head further south** through the steppe-like countryside marked by volcanic cones. After passing by ④ **Tindaya**, the holy mountain of the indigenous people, you will come to ⑤ **Tefía**, which is nowadays home to an open-air museum **Ecomuseo de la Alcogida** (Tue–Sat 10am–6pm | admission 5 euros) featuring restored farmhouses, mills and granaries. Another open-air museum with a beautifully restored mill and estate **Molino de Antigua** (Tue–Sat 10am–6pm | admission 2 euros) plus a cheese museum (Casa del Queso) awaits as you ap-

④ Tindaya
9 km/5.6 mi

⑤ Tefía
17 km/10.5 mi

proach ⑥ Antigua. Behind this village, the countryside becomes more mountainous. **The road winds up over bends and bare crests** to the most spectacular viewing platform ⑦ **Mirador Morro Velosa** at a height of almost 650 m (2133 ft). **At the two gigantic figures** – artistic representations of the last ancient Canarian rulers – **turn left** and you will shortly arrive at a kind of country estate with a fantastic **viewing terrace** (Tue–Sun 10am–6pm | free admission). On a clear day, you can see as far as Lanzarote, Gran Canaria and Tenerife!

01:00pm After some hairpin bends, make your way down to the former island capital of ⑧ Betancuria. Despite the fortress-like cathedral, several stately homes and the ruins of a monastery, the town has all the charm of a sleepy village. Make sure to visit the Casa Santa María (Mon–Sat 11am–3:30pm | admission 6 euros | www.casasantamaria. net), which is an exemplary restored house with traditional craftsmen's workshops, a garden café and a restaurant. **After leaving Betancuria, drive past** ⑨ Vega de Río Palmas, a palm tree oasis with a pilgrimage church. The appeal of the countryside grows even more as you look out over red mountains studded with furrows caused by erosion and isolated valleys in which hardly any plants thrive. If you have enough time, you might want to **take a detour from Pájara to the coastal village of Ajuy** (an additional 20 km (12.4 miles)) because the contrast between the white weathered limestone walls and the black lava beach is amazing. **Otherwise, follow the seemingly endless string of valleys and peaks straight to** ⑩ La Pared. White sand blows over the narrow isthmus that runs for 5 km (3.1 miles) from here to the eastern side of the island. **Now you need to head north** to make sure that you catch the last ferry back to Lanzarote. Additional places worth visiting include the zoo and botanical gardens of ⑪ Oasis Park (daily 9am–6pm | admission 33 euros | Ctra. FV-2, km 57.6 | www.fuerteventuraoasispark. com) in La Lajita, the salt marshes of the ⑫ Museo de la Sal (Tue–Sat 10am–6pm | admission 5 euros) at the Salinas del Carmen and the capital of ⑬ Puerto del Rosario with is lovely promenade along the sea.

04:00pm The last stretch of the route over the **FV-1 crosses the dunes** to bring you back to your starting point on Fuerteventura marked by white sand and the crystal-clear sea. Go for a swim or stroll through the old town centre of ⑭ **Corralejo** before your ferry departs for ① **Playa Blanca** → p. 76.

8 km/5 mi

⑦ Mirador Morro Velosa

3 km/1.9 mi

⑧ Betancuria

6 km/3.75 mi

⑨ Vega de Río Palmas

50 km/31 mi

⑩ La Pared

11 km/6.8 mi

⑪ Oasis Park

45 km/28 mi

⑫ Museo de la Sal

16 km/10 mi

⑬ Puerto del Rosario

32 k__/__ mi

⑭ Corralejo

14 km/8.5 mi

① Playa Blanca

SPORTS & ACTIVITIES

Because a constant wind is pretty well guaranteed, windsurfing is the number one water activity on Lanzarote. But given the good thermal currents, paragliding and hang gliding have also gained in popularity.

Lanzarote is also a great destination for cyclists and hikers. The guided walks in the Timanfaya National Park leave a lasting impression. Diving schools run courses and organise dives at interesting locations like the Museo Atlántico de Lanzarote off the coast at Playa Blanca. And then there's golf, riding, fishing and deep-sea fishing. If that is not enough, many holiday centres have tennis and squash courts. Other special events include (usually from May to December) beach volleyball tournaments, cy-

cle races and marathon running. One competition that attracts international attention is Ironman Lanzarote, where athletes have to swim 3.8 km, cycle 180 km round the island and finally run a marathon *(www.ironmanlanzarote.com)*.

CYCLING

The weather on Lanzarote is perfect year-round for all two-wheel enthusiasts. You can safely leave your waterproof clothing at home. Much more important is a plentiful supply of sunblock and a pair of sunglasses. A light windcheater is recommended for the cooler north and for early mornings and evenings. The hilly north of the magnificent volcanic landscape around Costa Teguise is ideal for

On land, on water, on a windsurfing board or a mountain bike: there are plenty of opportunities for action on and around this island

mountain bikers. But it is strictly forbidden to leave the (generally very good) trails. Racing cyclists and tourers will find near-perfect conditions throughout the island. No mountains are higher than 600 m (1975 ft). Cyclists will discover countless natural phenomena and scenic attractions on their travels, for example along the south-east coast.

Playa Blanca: *Cool Bikes (mountain bikes from 16 euros/day; E-Bikes and scooters | C/ el Correíllo 48 | tel. 9 28 51 77 87 | www. coolbikes.es)*

Costa Teguise: *Tommy's Bike Station (mountain bike 16–25 euros/day | Av. Islas Canarias 12 | C. C. Las Maretas 20B | to the right of the post office | mobile tel. 6 28 10 21 77 | www.tommys-bikes.com)* hires out excellent mountain bikes and offers INSIDER TIP free delivery of bikes to your holiday hotel.

Puerto del Carmen: Several bike hire points; a good choice and centrally located: *Renner Bikes (mountain bikes from 12 euros/day, racing bikes from 19 euros/ day | Centro Comercial Marítimo 25 Alto |*

tel. 928 51 06 12 | www.mountainbike-lanzarote.com).

DIVING

The underwater fauna off the Canary Islands is interesting and varied. One of the most memorable dives is INSIDER TIP on the coast near La Mala. Countless stingrays and eagle rays live on the seabed in the clear water. All diving schools request a one-off contribution of 12 euros for the decompression chamber in Arrecife.

Costa Teguise: The *Aquatis Diving Centre Lanzarote (dive 30 euros, with equipment 40 euros | Playa de las Cucharas, Local 6 | tel. 928 59 04 07 | www.diving-lanzarote.net)* offers dives and lessons (also to children).

Playa Blanca: Many courses and dives on offer at *Rubicon Diving (10 dives 420 euros | Marina Rubicón | Local 77b | tel. 928 34 93 46 | www.rubicondiving.com)*.

Puerto del Carmen: The Playa de la Barilla near the old harbour is the starting point for many dives. One popular underwater attraction is the *Catedral*, a 20 m/65 ft lava bubble in a vertical wall. *Safari Diving (dive with complete equipment 39 euros, 10 dives 337 euros | Playa de la Barrilla 4 | tel. 928 51 19 92 | www.safaridiving.com; Island Watersports (Av. del Varadero 36 | Marina | tel. 928 51 18 80 | www.divelanzarote.com)* includes in its programme dives from 30 euros, ten dives cost 246 euros.

GOLF

A semidesert with lush carpets of green grass behind an ocean of blue: Lanzarote's golf courses are breathtakingly beautiful! The 18-hole course of *Golf Costa Teguise (daily 8am–8pm | greenfee 70 euros | tel. 9 28 59 05 12 | www.lanzarote-golf.com)* looks back on a long tradition. Also attractive: the newer 18 hole course *Lanzarote Golf (daily 8am–8pm |*

Step by step: the sparse volcanic landscape slowly clears the mind

greenfee 75 euros | access via LZ-505 | tel. 9 28 51 40 50 | www.lanzarotegolfresort. com) near Puerto del Carmen.

HANG GLIDING

The preferred launch-pad for hang gliders is the 502 m (1650 ft) Montaña Tinasoria near Puerto del Carmen. Lift-offs are also possible from various points on the Risco de Famara and near Mala. But take care. The thermals on Lanzarote can be very strong and unpredictable changes in wind direction are frequent. There have already been many serious accidents, so beginners should only take off under expert supervision (e.g. with *www.volcanofly-lanzarote.com* and *www.lanzarote-tandemflights.com)*!

HIKING

Lanzarote is not an island known for hiking, but there are some marked trails. The area around the Parque Nacional de Timanfaya in particular is a great place to explore on foot (see p. 74). Hiking tours around the Fire Mountains are also organised by *Lanzatrekk (www.lanzatrekk.com).*

STAND-UP-PADDLING

SUP is offered in all the resort areas. You can rent the necessary equipment and take lessons in Costa Teguise at *SUP Lanzarote (Playa de los Charcos | www.suplanzarote.com); in Puerto del Carmen at Lava Flow Surf (www.lavaflowsurf.com);* and in Playa Blanca at *Kaboti Surf (www. kabotisurf.com).*

SURFING

Experienced surfers with short boards reckon the conditions off Playa de Famara, which sees high, long-breaking waves, rank among the best on the island. But caution is advised. There are some dangerous currents in these parts. *Costa Noroeste (course from 35 euros/half day | Av. El Marinero 11 | La Caleta de Famara | tel. 9 28 52 85 97 | www.costanoroeste.com).*

WELLNESS

All four and five-star hotels offer spas with hydro-massage pools, jacuzzis, saunas and steam baths. Sometimes these services are not included in the room price. Massages and other wellness services almost always cost extra. The *Hotel Princesa Yaiza* (see p. 80) has the best spa, followed by *Gran Castillo Tagoro* (see p. 81) and *The Hotel Volcán Lanzarote* (see p. 81) in Playa Blanca. The sprawling spa in the hotel *Costa Calero* (see p. 70) in Puerto Calero has a lazy river that will carry you from the indoor pool out into the fresh air.

WINDSURFING

The best places for windsurfing are Costa Teguise and La Caleta de Famara. International competitions are staged on the turbulent waters renowned for their capricious currents off the Famara beaches as well as in Costa Teguise.

Costa Teguise: Strong side winds blow on the Playa de las Cucharas. *Windsurf Paradise (C/ la Corvina 8 | tel. 6 35 05 41 10 | www.windsurflanzarote.com)* and the *Windsurfing Club* (see p. 44) offer very good facilities. Boards cost from 40 euros per day to hire, beginners' courses from 90 euros.

At *Calima Surf (Av. El Marinero 13 | tel. 9 28 52 85 28 | www.calimasurf.com)* in La Caleta de Famara, watersports services on offer include the loan of windsurfing boards and windsurfing and surfing lessons, and also lessons in kitesurfing.

TRAVEL WITH KIDS

Younger guests are important guests. There are children's pools and play-grounds in almost all of the holiday complexes; supermarkets stock all baby requirements, e.g. food, toys, dispos-able nappies.

Before booking a hotel or apartment, make sure it is within easy reach of the beach. Family hotels usually offer a full service for children: supervision, anima-tion with games, sports, play, shows and children's discos (enquire when book-ing). In addition, there will always be high chairs in the restaurants and free cots in the rooms/apartments.

One of Lanzarote's five-star hotels showcases itself as being especially child-friendly. The *Hotel Princesa Yaiza* in Playa Blanca has spacious rooms that could almost be described as suites and include a kitchenette. In addition, there is a baby club, a mini club and a junior club for older children. Hotel guests have free access to the 10,000 sq m *Kikoland* (see p. 107) with bouncy castles and water slides, adventure playground and entertainers dressed as fairy-tale characters. Your children will quickly find friends of their own age.

The sheltered beaches at Puerto del Carmen and Playa Blanca are perfect for youngsters, as there are no high waves or strong currents. More care is needed in Costa Teguise, because the winds and waves are stronger there. Only Playa del Jablillo is suitable for younger children. Parents should avoid altogether Playa de Famara, because of

Pools of their own, playgrounds, shows, there's even a children's park: youngsters holidaying on Lanzarote can never get bored

the choppy inshore waters and unpredictable currents.

For Spanish children, the highlight of Christmas is not Christmas Day but Epiphany (6 January). They receive their Christmas presents on the morning of *Reyes Magos*. True to the story of the Nativity, on Lanzarote the Three Kings arrive on camels. At carnival time at the start of Lent, children have their own festivals and crown their own *reina de carnaval*, the carnival queen.

COSTA TEGUISE AND THE NORTH

AQUAPARK

(129 E4) *(㊙ G9)*

Apart from hotel pools, the freshwater swimming pool below the golf course in Costa Teguise is the only alternative to the sea. There are a dozen water slides, several pools, paddling pools, trampoline, mini-scooter and an (adventure) playground. However, there is also some criticism from parents: some say the water is too cold, supervision is inadequate and admission prices are inflated. *Daily 10am–6pm (only open in the summer) | admission 20 euros, children 15 euros, loungers 2.50 euros | Av. del Golf | aqua parklanzarote.es*

glass tunnel above the visitors. You can even observe fish embryos growing in the egg. *Daily 10am–6pm | admission 14 euros, children 9 euros | Av. Las Acacias | Centro Comercial El Trébol | www.aquar iumlanzarote.com*

A big splash landing awaits at the end of the slides at Aqualava Waterpark

GRANJA LAS PARDELAS
(129 E3) (*Ø H5*)

Small petting zoo with goats, rabbits, a horse and donkeys. Rides are offered on the latter. Kids can make their own pottery to remember the day. *Daily 10am–6pm | La Quemadita 88 | Órzola | admission 4.50 euros, children 3.50 euros, donkey ride 3.50 euros | tel. 9 28 84 25 45 | www.pardelas-park.com*

LANZAROTE AQUARIUM ●
(129 E4) (*Ø G9*)

About 20 well-illuminated tanks re-create the habitats of many sea creatures, among them sea cucumbers, spider crabs, clownfish, moray eels and rays. Mussels are bred in lava pools, sharks swim in a

MUSEO DE LA PIRATERÍA (PIRATE MUSEUM) (129 D2) (*Ø F7*)

You'll think of knights and brigands as soon as you see the Castillo de Santa Bárbara. Model ships, canons and other weapons tell of the many times that Lanzarote was attacked by pirates. *Daily 10am–3:30pm | admission 3 euros, children free | www.museodelapirateria.com*

PUERTO DEL CARMEN AND THE CENTRE

LANZAROTE A CABALLO
(131 D4) (*Ø C10*)

At this small horse ranch outside Uga, children up to age 8 can ride ponies. Older kids can ride "proper" horses or even dromedaries. *Daily | 1 hour riding lesson 40 euros | Ctra. Arrecife–Yaiza km 17 | tel. 9 28 83 00 38 | www.lanzaroteaca ballo.com*

RANCHO TEXAS LANZAROTE PARK
(131 F4) (*⌂ D10*)
This former horse ranch has been expanded to include an adventure and animal park. Among the creatures are turtles, lizards, bison, deer, pumas, armadillos and raccoons. The white tigers attract a lot of attention. Children love to play in the Sioux village and are thrilled by the performances of the parrots, raptors and sea lions. They can search for gold treasure and go canoeing. Once or twice a week there's a *Western night (Tue, Fri, Sat 7pm–11pm | admission 38 euros, children 20 euros | tel. 928 84 12 86)* with entertainment and barbecue. On these nights, shuttle buses operate between the park and holiday resorts (free from Puerto del Carmen). *Daily 9:30am–5:30pm | admission 25 euros, children (2–14 years) 20 euros | leave Puerto del Carmen on C/ Noruega and cross under the bypass | www.ranchotexaslanzarote.com*

TIMANFAYA NATIONAL PARK

DROMEDARY STATION (126 C5) (*⌂ C9*)
The most exotic experience on Lanzarote is certainly a ride through the fields of black lava in the Timanfaya National Park on a dromedary. If you specifically ask, smaller children can usually ride on the back of the animal, with parents in the seats on the right and left. Youngsters get closer to these hard-working animals at the dromedary station on the edge of Timanfaya National Park. Suitable for children from 3 years. *Mon–Fri 9am–3pm (duration approx. 20 minutes) | 8 euros per person | Echadero de los Camellos*

PLAYA BLANCA

AQUALAVA WATERPARK
(130 B6) (*⌂ B12*)
Water slides, wet castles, a lazy river and artificial waves can be found just behind the beach of Playa Flamingo. *Daily | admission 20 euros, childrern 10 euros | C/ Gran Canaria 26 | behind the Playa Flamingo, in the complex Relaxia Lanzasur | www.aqualava.net*

BOAT TRIPS
(130 B6) (*⌂ B12*)
Gliding along on the water – an outing that will put not only the children in a good mood! On days when the ocean is calm, the harbour of Playa Blanca becomes the starting point for a number of different tours. Boats from *Líneas Romero (express waterbus 15 euros, children 8 euros | www.lineasromero.com)* sail to the Playas de Papagayo, where you can swim and snorkel. Or you can go watch whales and dolphins from the deck of a sailing ship *(tour 75 euros, children 50 euros | www.cetaceosynavegacion. com)*. The underwater world leisurely glides by beneath the ● glass-bottom boats of Líneas Romero as they head for the neighbouring island of Fuerteventura *(incl. time on shore and snorkelling break 44 euros, children 25 euros)*. The little ferry of the same operator sets course for Fuerteventura several times a day *(ticket 27 euros, children 15 euros)*.

KIKOLAND
(130 B6) (*⌂ B12*)
Attractions at this sports and children's playground include several pools, bouncy castle, loungers and lots more. It is suitable for youngsters from 3 years of age under parental supervision. *Daily 10am–6pm | admission for families 24 euros | next to the Hotel Princesa Yaiza*

FESTIVALS & EVENTS

First the procession, then the party: Nearly all festivals on Lanzarote have a religious origin, be it the veneration of a patron saint or the commemoration of a miracle. The image of a saint is carried through the streets, with rather doleful tunes and chanting, such as the *folías*, reflecting the island's barren land. But the highlight of every festival has to be the party. Salsa and rock music resonate around the alleyways, and everyone joins in – whether aged eight or 80.

Festivals, concerts and theatrical events are staged in the INSIDER TIP spectacular cave auditorium of Jameos del Agua throughout the year. The only occasional INSIDER TIP concerts in the auditorium at the Cueva de los Verdes are just as atmospheric. Information and tickets from the tourist office and *www.centrosturisticos. com.*

FESTIVALS & EVENTS

6 JANUARY

The Three Kings **Los Reyes Magos** ride through Arrecife and other towns and villages on the island on dromedaries, receiving an enthusiastic welcome from the children, who have been waiting excitedly to receive their presents.

FEBRUARY/MARCH

⭐ *Carnaval:* The wildest celebration of all starts at the end of January and can go on until early March. Every place has its own dates for the Carnaval festivities and processions. The highlights are the events in Puerto del Carmen, Haría and Arrecife.

MARCH/APRIL

The processions in Arrecife during the **Semana Santa** or Holy Week are extravagant celebrations.

MAY

Ironman Lanzarote: Swim, bike and run at this annual triathlon competition

MAY/JUNE

Corpus Christi: Catholic processions in Arrecife and Haría

24 JUNE

INSIDER TIP *Fiesta de San Juan*: Festival to celebrate the harvest and summer solstice, dating back to the aboriginal settlers. On the eve of the fiesta in Haría, camp-fires are lit and scarecrows burnt.

Festivals on Lanzarote combine religion and folklore. Carnival is always an extravagant celebration

JULY

Wine festivals in Masdache and other places in the vine-growing area of La Geria to music and dancing.

7 JULY

Fiesta de San Marcial del Rubicón: In Femés a week of processions, honouring the patron saint of Lanzarote.

16 JULY

Fiesta de Nuestra Señora del Carmen: processions are held in Playa Blanca, Puerto del Carmen and La Graciosa to commemorate the patron saint of fishermen.

8 SEPTEMBER

With processions and folklórico events, Yaiza pays its respects to its saint during the *Fiesta de la Virgen de los Remedios*.

15 SEPTEMBER

Romería de Mancha Blanca: Festival in honour of the *Virgen de los Dolores,* Our Lady of Sorrows.

24 DECEMBER

⭐ *Fiesta de los Ranchos de Pascua:* After midnight, folklore and music in Teguise; nativity scene in Yaiza.

NATIONAL HOLIDAYS

1 Jan	*Año Nuevo* (New Year)
6 Jan	*Los Reyes*
March/April	*Viernes Santo*
1 May	*Día del Trabajo*
30 May	*Día de las Islas Canarias*
May/June	*Corpus Christi*
25 July	*Santiago Apóstol*
15 Aug	*Asunción*
12 Oct	Day of the discovery of America
1 November	*Todos los Santos*
6 Dec	Constitution Day
8 Dec	*Inmaculada Concepción*
25 Dec	*Navidad*

LINKS, BLOGS, APPS & MORE

www.lanzaroteinformation.com By far the best source of information about Lanzarote on the web. Everything from where to find the best flight deals to advice on relocating to Lanzarote; blogs

www.cactlanzarote.com César Manrique's landscape art and other top attractions

ociolanzarote.com Information, pictures and a film about Lanzarote's carnival (click "Eventos Tradicionales", in Spanish)

www.memoriadelanzarote.com The island's "digital memory". Text, audio and video clips are only available in Spanish, but the countless pictures documenting Lanzarote's history will be of interest to all, even if the language poses problems

www.masscultura.com An easy-to-navigate website mainly in Spanish showcasing forthcoming cultural events in the world of literature, music and art. Also available as pdf to download and print

www.surfbirds.com You will find all native bird species of Lanzarote in this English-speaking community – and can directly send any of the photographs as a postcard

www.outdoorlanzarote.com A collection of mainly medium-length walks on Lanzarote with expert advice and photos

www.danistein.com A blog by photographer Dani Stein, who lives on Lanzarote. Do check out this site. You will be amazed by the quality of the photos posted there – ideal for getting into the right island mood

www.bloglanzarote.wordpress.com Blog with evocative photos, not regularly updated anymore, but still informative

lanzarotetouristnetwork.com Lanzarote information by people who know Lanzarote. A popular site. Need to know

Regardless of whether you are still preparing your trip or already on Lanzarote: these addresses will provide you with more information, videos and networks to make your holiday even more enjoyable

more about a hotel or a resort, then someone here will be able to help you

www.lanzarotegayguide.com and www.gaylanza.com News and information from the island's gay scene. Advice on gay bars, both with forum

www.youtube.com/watch?v= q9hxz-OKb-n0 "The Lanzarote Effect": short video on Lanzarote with interesting and beautiful effects

VIDEOS & MUSIC

www.youtube.com/watch?v=ReF_zoxV_7k&list=TLdRegyWF66hw This video is called "Tierra, Agua y Fuego" ("Earth, Water and Fire") and shows Lanzarote from a bird's-eye view

www.rtve.es/alacarta/videos/imprescindibles/imprescindibles-taro-eco-man rique/3561244 This hour-long film of the series "The Indispensables" was produced by Spanish national television and presents the life and work of the ubiquitous island artist César Manrique. It openly discusses Lanzarote's environmental sins – but is, unfortunately, only available in Spanish

www.lanzaroteinformation.com/content/radio-stations-lanzarote There are three English-language stations on Lanzarote, UK Away FM Buzz FM and Holiday FM. Choose your preferred listening from this link. Plus other Spanish stations

Lanzarote App Free app with event calendar, sights, videos and pictures

APPS

Lanzarote!2go App issued by the island's government containing all important sights

Star Walk Lanzarote is the perfect place for stargazing as long as you move away from the main resorts. This app will guide you through the galaxies

The Kite and Windsurfing Navigator Up-to-date forecasts and wind alerts for water sports enthusiasts. Now a free iPhone app

GuaguApp App by Lanzarote's bus network with all bus timetables on the island

TRAVEL TIPS

ACCOMODATION

From five-star hotels to inns, from simple apartments to luxury villas: Lanzarote offers a wide range of accommodations. This is not only true for the tourist resorts, but is becoming more common on the interior of the island as well. There are also a large number of privately owned rentals, but their rates are now on par with those of hotels or apartments. As a general rule: be sure to make your reservations far enough in advance – the Canary Islands have become very popular since wars and crises have broken out in North Africa and the Middle East.

ARRIVAL

Cheap flights are available from the UK and Ireland with Ryanair, easyjet and Thomas Cook (flight time from UK approx. 4 hours). Flights with no hotel booking cost between 300 and 500 euros. Scheduled flights are much more expensive and nearly always involve a stopover. There are no direct flights from the USA.

Lanzarote's airport is a drive of between 10 and 30 minutes from the main holiday centres. At busy times there is a direct bus into Arrecife every 30 minutes *(no. 22/23),* to Puerto del Carmen and Playa Blanca every hour *(no. 161/61).* Taxis to Puerto del Carmen cost approx. 22 euros, to Costa Teguise 28 euros and to Playa Blanca about 50 euros.

In case you want to bring your own car: There are ferries leaving from the southern Spanish mainland port of Cádiz once a week. The Compañía Acciona Trasmediterránea operates a car ferry service, with a crossing taking 30 to 35 hours to Arrecife. A car can cost 380 euros (one way). To book a crossing either visit a travel agency or go online *(www.trasmediterranea.es).*

RESPONSIBLE TRAVEL

It doesn't take a lot to be environmentally friendly whilst travelling. Don't just think about your carbon footprint whilst flying to and from your holiday destination but also about how you can protect nature and culture abroad. As a tourist it is especially important to respect nature, look out for local products, cycle instead of driving, save water and much more. If you would like to find out more about eco-tourism please visit: *www.ecotourism.org*

BEACHES

The beaches at the holiday resorts are well equipped: you can rent umbrellas and loungers, lifeguards keep a watchful eye on the water fun and there is a local Red Cross Station for emergencies. Free (foot) showers and restroom facilities are provided and the next pub is never far away. However, things are very different at the so-called natural beaches outside of the resorts – be sure to take along everything you will need. Most beaches don't even provide a lifebuoy. Keep in mind that the currents and surf on the western side of the island are dangerously strong, which is why you shouldn't do more than just dip in your toes. However, treacherous waves and unexpected rip currents can even develop on the calmer eastern side – be sure to pay attention to the warning flags.

BUSES

Scheduled buses (*guaguas*) leave for all the larger villages (but often only once or twice a day) from the bus station in Arrecife, the *Estación de Guaguas (Vía Medular | near the stadium | tel. 928 811 5 22 | www.arrecifebus.com)*. All the main tourist centres are served by buses: Puerto del Carmen (no. 2) and Costa Teguise (no. 1) Mon–Fri every 20 minutes, Sat–Sun every 30 minutes, Playa Blanca (no. 6 and 60) Mon–Fri about every hour, Sat and Sun six to eight times a day.

A small, but INSIDER TIP much more centrally located bus terminal can be found at the western end of the Playa del Reducto in Arrecife. Buses serve Puerto del Carmen, Playa Blanca and the airport. If you want to take the bus a lot, buy a rechargeable *tarjeta sin contacto (Bono Bus Lanzarote)* which makes fares cheaper by ten per cent or more. The tourist information tells you where to buy it.

CAMPING

Camping de Papagayo (Playa de Puerto Muelas | you must reserve ahead by phone: 9 28 17 37 24), the campsite in Playa Blanca, is only open in summer. On the neighbouring island of La Graciosa, to the south of Caleta del Sebo, there is a campsite on the Bahía de El Salado with showers and toilets. Information and an online reservation form (two months in advance at the earliest) can be found on *www.reservasparquesnacionales.es.*

CAR HIRE

Car hire companies have offices in Arrecife, at the airport and in all the holiday centres. The cheapest local company is *Cabrera Medina (tel. 9 28 82 29 00| www.cabreramedina.com),* which also has the most branches and well-maintained cars – if there is any problem, they will provide you with a new car straight away. As the company also operates on Fuerteventura, you can also easily book a car if you plan to take a side trip to this neighbouring island. This will save you the cost of paying to have your hire car transported by ferry. If you book online, you can hire a small car (such as a Corsa) for less than 140 euros per week.

BUDGETING

Meal	from £ 7 /$ 9.40
	for the dish of the day and a drink in a basic restaurant frequented by locals
Coffee	from £ 1.33 /$ 1.77
	for a cortado
Beach lounger	£ 5.30 /$ 7
	per day
Wine	from £ 5.30 /$ 7
	for a half-litre carafe of wine
Petrol	about £ 0.89 /$ 1.18
	for one litre of Eurosuper
Aloe vera	approx. £ 14 /$ 19
	for 250 ml aloe vera gel (100 per cent)

CLIMATE, WHEN TO GO

The climate on Lanzarote is mild. However, in the summer it can get oppressively hot, while winter evenings are quite cool because of the constant trade winds. The best times to visit are the moderately warm months from November to March. During the holiday months of July and August and around Easter, many mainland Spaniards visit the island.

CONSULATES & EMBASSIES

UK CONSULATE
C/ Luis Morote 6-3º | Las Palmas de Gran Canaria | tel. 928 26 25 08 | www.ukin spain.fco.gov.uk

US CONSULATE
Edificio ARCA | C/ Los Martínez Escobar, 3, Oficina 7 | 35007 Las Palmas | tel. 928 2712 59 | madrid.usembassy.gov/ citizen-services/offices/las-palmas.html

CUSTOMS

If you arrive on the Canary Islands from an EU country, no customs checks are necessary. The Canary Islands have a special duty-free tax status and so, as a result, items such as alcohol, tobacco and perfume are cheaper here than in mainland Spain or the rest onf Europe. Duty-free allowances for anyone over 17 are as follows: 200 cigarettes or 50 cigars or 250 g tobacco, other goods up to a value of 430 euros (children under 15: 175 euros), 1 litre of spirits, 2 litres of wine.

EMERGENCY SERVICES

Dial 112 for emergencies of all kinds, e.g. police, fire, ambulance, accident.

HEALTH

It is easy for visitors to misjudge the physical strains that the change in climate places on the body, particularly at the height of summer. Tap water is not drinkable; all supermarkets sell mineral water in plastic bottles of 5 to 8 litres.

DOCTORS
The European Health Insurance Card (EHIC) entitles citizens of countries in the

LIVING ON THE LAND: TURISMO RURAL

Spend your holiday in the country among the locals! These historic country houses *(casas rurales)* far off from the tourist centres offer comfortable rooms with all the amenities – perfect for families. Another plus: the rates are often lower than those of hotels. The houses are usually rented out by the week. A rental car is an absolute must for getting around because bus services are few and far between when you get away from the tourist hubs.

But no matter where on Lanzarote you want to go, the site *www.littlehotels. co.uk/canaries/lanzarote.php* has a small, charming hotel for you! Or, if you are looking for a **INSIDER TIP** rural, family-owned accommodation off the beaten track, look at *www.responsibletravel. com/holidays/lanzarote/travel-guide/ru ral-accommodation-in-lanzarote*. Further websites are *www.fincas-lanzarote.com/ cottage* and *www.bungalowfamara.com*.

European Union to free treatment from doctors who are part of the Spanish Seguridad Social scheme. When paying for medical care, ask for a detailed invoice *(factura)*, which you can present to your insurance company when you return home.

PHARMACIES

If you need a pharmacy *(farmacia)* look out for the green cross outside. *Opening times: Mon–Fri 9am–1:30pm and 4–8:30 pm, Sat 9am–1pm.* The sign with the words "Farmacia de Guardia" refers to the nearest pharmacy open for emergencies.

INFORMATION BEFORE YOU LEAVE

SPANISH NATIONAL TOURISM OFFICES

www.spain.info, tel (*) 00 800 10 10 50 50
– 6th Floor 64 North Row | W1K 7DE London | info.londres@tourspain.es
– 1395 Brickell Avenue, Suite 1130 | Miami, FL 33131 | oetmiami@tourspain.es
– 845 North Michigan Av, Suite 915-E | Chicago, IL 60611 | chicago@tourspain.es
– 8383 Wilshire Blvd., Suite 956 | Beverly Hills, CA 90211 | losangeles@tourspain.es
– 60 East 42nd Street, Suite 5300 (53rd Floor) | New York, NY 10165-0039 | nuevayork@tourspain.es

INFORMATION ON LANZAROTE

Brochures, maps and information are available at the tourist offices in Arrecife, Puerto del Carmen, Playa Blanca, Costa Teguise and Teguise (see the heading "information" in every region chapter of this guide), as well as at the airport. The website *www.turismolanzarote.com* has information on nature, culture, beaches and the sea, sports and local events.

INTERNET & WIFI

Almost all the hotels on the island offer WiFi or LAN internet access, but the price is not always included with your accommodation. Free public hotspots are rather difficult to find. Look for the "WiFi" signs in cafés and bars where you can usually use the internet for free as long as you order something.

INTERNET CAFÉS

Internet cafés can be found in amusement arcades *(salones recreativos)* in all tourist centres.
– Cibercafé Internet (daily 10am–midnight | Av. de las Playas 30 | Puerto del Carmen)
– Internet café (daily 10am–midnight | promenade near the Restaurant Almacén de la Sal | Playa Blanca)

LANGUAGE

You can get by without knowing any Spanish if you stay at a hotel at one of the tourist resorts. However, if you want to order something at Canarian restaurants off the beaten track or even want to tour the island by bus, you should at least know some basic Spanish. We have put together a few important words and phrases in our phrase book on page 118.

MEDIA

There are three English-language stations on Lanzarote, UK Away FM, Buzz FM and Holiday FM. English newspapers and magazines are sold in the main holiday centres.

MONEY & CREDIT CARDS

ATMs or cash machines are an inexpensive way to withdraw cash from your account. Note that cards with PIN numbers longer than 4 digits will not work in Spain. Check also the fees you will be charged for withdrawing foreign currency. Credit cards are accepted in almost all hotels, shops, restaurants and service stations. Bank opening times: *Mon–Fri 8:30am–2pm, Sat 8:30am–1pm*.

PHONE & MOBILE PHONE

The dialling code for Spain: 0034 if calling from either the UK or Ireland, 01134 from the USA, followed by the nine-digit number (including the area code 928). Roaming charges were abolished within the EU in 2017. Therefore, if you are an EU resident, you should not be charged higher rates for calls anywhere in the EU. For travellers from the US and Canada, many providers offer travel packages for international destinations. You can also phone home from one of the (rare) phone boxes. Most *internacional* boxes take coins and phone cards *(teletarjeta)*. These can be purchased at newspaper kiosks for 6 or 12 euros. In the holiday centres, you will find call shops *(locutorio)*, where the caller is billed for the call when it is terminated.

UK dialling code: 0044: USA dialling code: 001. This is followed by the local area code without the zero and the number you are calling.

CURRENCY CONVERTER

£	€	€	£
1	1.40	1	0.72
3	4.17	3	2.15
5	6.96	5	3.59
13	18.08	13	9.34
40	55.65	40	28.75
75	104	75	53.89
120	167	120	86
250	348	250	180
500	696	500	359

$	€	€	$
1	0.92	1	1.09
3	2.75	3	3.27
5	4.58	5	5.45
13	11.92	13	14.18
40	36.67	40	43.64
75	69	75	81.82
120	110	120	131
250	229	250	273
500	458	500	545

For current exchange rates see www.xe.com

POST

Stamps *(sellos)* are sold at the post office *(correos)* as well as at the *estancos,* the tobacconist's shops. A letter *(carta)* or a postcard *(postal)* to countries within the EU requires a stamp costing 1.25 euros.

PRICES

A beer in a bar for the locals is likely to cost around 1.50 euros, a tapa from 3 euros and the dish of the day 5 from euros. The same items will probably cost twice that amount in a bar in one of the holiday centres.

TAXI

Taxis on Lanzarote carry a roof sign with a green light and number, plus the letters SP on the number plate. All taxis must be licensed and equipped with a taximeter, which must be switched on before every journey. The basic charge is between 2.30 and 3 euros (depending on whether you're in the country or in the city), then 1 euro for every further kilometre plus surcharges for night drives as well as start or ending of the trip at the airport or the ferry port. If you hire a taxi to take you on a round-the-island tour, make sure you agree a price beforehand.

TIME

Unlike mainland Spain, Lanzarote runs on Greenwich Mean Time, so visitors from the UK and Ireland do not need to adjust their watches.

TIPPING

In restaurants, it is customary to leave a tip of 5 to 10 per cent of the bill. However, you should only give a tip if you were really satisfied with the service.

Lizards are hard to detect on the lava fields

WEATHER IN ARRECIFE

	Jan	Feb	March	April	May	June	July	Aug	Sept	Oct	Nov	Dec
Daytime temperatures in °C/°F	21/70	22/72	23/73	23/73	23/73	25/77	28/82	29/84	29/84	27/81	25/77	20/68
Nighttime temperatures in °C/°F	13/55	13/55	14/57	14/57	15/59	16/61	18/64	18/64	18/64	19/66	16/61	14/57
☀ Sunshine hours/day	6	7	8	9	9	9	9	9	7	7	6	6
☂ Precipitation days/month	3	2	2	1	0	0	0	0	1	1	4	5
〜 Water temperature in °C/°F	18/64	18/64	17/63	17/63	18/64	20/68	20/68	21/70	22/72	22/72	20/68	19/66

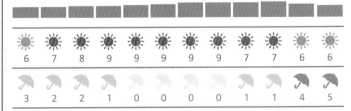

USEFUL PHRASES SPANISH

PRONUNCIATION

c	before "e" and "i" like "th" in "thin"
ch	as in English
g	before "e" and "i" like the "ch" in Scottish "loch"
gue, gui	like "get", "give"
que, qui	the "u" is not spoken, i.e. "ke", "ki"
j	always like the "ch" in Scottish "loch"
ll	like "ll'" in "million"; some speak it like "y" in "yet"
ñ	"nj"
z	like "th" in "thin"

IN BRIEF

Yes/No/Maybe	sí/no/quizás
Please/Thank you	por favor/gracias
Hello!/Goodbye!/See you	¡Hola!/¡Adiós!/¡Hasta luego!
Good morning!/afternoon!/evening!/night!	¡Buenos días!/¡Buenos días!/¡Buenas tardes!/¡Buenas noches!
Excuse me, please!	¡Perdona!/¡Perdone!
May I...?/Pardon?	¿Puedo...?/¿Cómo dice?
My name is...	Me llamo...
What's your name?	¿Cómo se llama usted?/¿Cómo te llamas?
I'm from...	Soy de...
I would like to.../Have you got...?	Querría.../¿Tiene usted...?
How much is...?	¿Cuánto cuesta...?
I (don't) like that	Esto (no) me gusta.
good/bad/broken/doesn't work	bien/mal/roto/no funciona
too much/much/little/all/nothing	demasiado/mucho/poco/todo/nada
Help!/Attention!/Caution!	¡Socorro!/¡Atención!/¡Cuidado!
ambulance/police/fire brigade	ambulancia/policía/bomberos
May I take a photo here	¿Podría fotografiar aquí?

DATE & TIME

Monday/Tuesday/Wednesday	lunes/martes/miércoles
Thursday/Friday/Saturday	jueves/viernes/sábado
Sunday/working day/holiday	domingo/laborable/festivo
today/tomorrow/yesterday	hoy/mañana/ayer

¿Hablas español?

"Do you speak Spanish?" This guide will help you to say the basic words and phrases in Spanish.

hour/minute/second/moment	hora/minuto/segundo/momento
day/night/week/month/year	día/noche/semana/mes/año
now/immediately/before/after	ahora/enseguida/antes/después
What time is it?	¿Qué hora es?
It's three o'clock/It's half past three	Son las tres/Son las tres y media
a quarter to four/a quarter past four	cuatro menos cuarto/ cuatro y cuarto

TRAVEL

open/closed/opening times	abierto/cerrado/horario
entrance / exit	entrada/acceso salida
departure/arrival	salida/llegada
toilets/ladies/gentlemen	aseos/señoras/caballeros
free/occupied	libre/ocupado
(not) drinking water	agua (no) potable
Where is...?/Where are...?	¿Dónde está...? /¿Dónde están...?
left/right	izquierda/derecha
straight ahead/back	recto/atrás
close/far	cerca/lejos
traffic lights/corner/crossing	semáforo/esquina/cruce
bus/tram/U-underground/taxi/cab	autobús/tranvía/metro/taxi
bus stop/cab stand	parada/parada de taxis
parking lot/parking garage	parking/garaje
street map/map	plano de la ciudad/mapa
train station/harbour/airport	estación/puerto/aeropuerto
ferry/quay	transbordador/muelle
schedule/ticket/supplement	horario/billete/suplemento
single/return	sencillo/ida y vuelta
train/track/platform	tren/vía/andén
delay/strike	retraso/huelga
I would like to rent...	Querría... alquilar
a car/a bicycle/a boat	un coche/una bicicleta/un barco
petrol/gas station	gasolinera
petrol/gas / diesel	gasolina/diesel
breakdown/repair shop	avería/taller

FOOD & DRINK

Could you please book a table for tonight for four?	Resérvenos, por favor, una mesa para cuatro personas para hoy por la noche.
on the terrace/by the window	en la terraza/junto a la ventana

The menu, please/	¡El menú, por favor!
Could I please have...?	¿Podría traerme... por favor?
bottle/carafe/glass	botella/jarra/vaso
knife/fork/spoon	cuchillo/tenedor/cuchara
salt/pepper/sugar	sal/pimienta/azúcar
vinegar/oil/milk/cream/lemon	vinagre/aceite/leche/limón
cold/too salty/not cooked	frío/demasiado salado/sin hacer
with/without ice/sparkling	con/sin hielo/gas
vegetarian/allergy	vegetariano/vegetariana/alergía
May I have the bill, please?	Querría pagar, por favor.
bill/receipt/tip	cuenta/recibo/propina

SHOPPING

pharmacy/chemist	farmacia/droguería
baker/market	panadería/mercado
butcher/fishmonger	carnicería/pescadería
shopping centre/department store	centro comercial/grandes almacenes
shop/supermarket/kiosk	tienda/supermercado/quiosco
100 grammes/1 kilo	cien gramos/un kilo
expensive/cheap/price/more/less	caro/barato/precio/más/menos
organically grown	de cultivo ecológico

ACCOMMODATION

I have booked a room	He reservado una habitación.
Do you have any... left?	¿Tiene todavía...?
single room/double room	habitación individual/habitación doble
breakfast/half board/	desayuno/media pensión/
full board (American plan)	pensión completa
at the front/seafront/garden view	hacia delante/hacia el mar/hacia el jardín
shower/sit-down bath	ducha/baño
balcony/terrace	balcón/terraza
key/room card	llave/tarjeta
luggage/suitcase/bag	equipaje/maleta/bolso
swimming pool/spa/sauna	piscina/spa/sauna
soap/toilet paper/nappy (diaper)	jabón/papel higiénico/pañal
cot/high chair/nappy changing	cuna/trona/cambiar los pañales
deposit	anticipo/caución

BANKS, MONEY & CREDIT CARDS

bank/ATM/	banco/cajero automático/
pin code	número secreto
cash/credit card	en efectivo/tarjeta de crédito
bill/coin/change	billete/moneda/cambio

HEALTH

doctor/dentist/paediatrician	médico/dentista/pediatra
hospital/emergency clinic	hospital/urgencias
fever/pain/inflamed/injured	fiebre/dolor/inflamado/herido
diarrhoea/nausea/sunburn	diarrea/náusea/quemadura de sol
plaster/bandage/ointment/cream	tirita/vendaje/pomada/crema
pain reliever/tablet/suppository	calmante/comprimido/supositorio

POST, TELECOMMUNICATIONS & MEDIA

stamp/letter/postcard	sello/carta/postal
I need a landline phone card/	Necesito una tarjeta telefónica/
I'm looking for a prepaid card for my mobile	Busco una tarjeta prepago para mi móvil
Where can I find internet access?	¿Dónde encuentro un acceso a internet?
dial/connection/engaged	marcar/conexión/ocupado
socket/adapter/charger	enchufe/adaptador/cargador
computer/battery/	ordenador/batería/
rechargeable battery	batería recargable
e-mail address/at sign (@)	(dirección de) correo electrónico/arroba
internet address (URL)	dirección de internet
internet connection/wifi	conexión a internet/wifi
e-mail/file/print	archivo/imprimir

LEISURE, SPORTS & BEACH

beach/sunshade/lounger	playa/sombrilla/tumbona
low tide/high tide/current	marea baja/marea alta/corriente

NUMBERS

0	cero	14	catorce
1	un, uno, una	15	quince
2	dos	16	dieciséis
3	tres	17	diecisiete
4	cuatro	18	dieciocho
5	cinco	19	diecinueve
6	seis	20	veinte
7	siete	100	cien, ciento
8	ocho	200	doscientos, doscientas
9	nueve	1000	mil
10	diez	2000	dos mil
11	once	10 000	diez mil
12	doce	1/2	medio
13	trece	1/4	un cuarto

ROAD ATLAS

The green line indicates the Discovery Tour "Lanzarote at a glance"
The blue line indicates the other Discovery Tours

All tours are also marked on the pull-out map

Photo: Waves break at Los Hervideros

Exploring Lanzarote

**The map on the back cover shows how the area
has been sub-divided**

	A	B	C

1

2 km
1.24 mi

Caletón Oscuro
ISLA DE MONTAÑA CLARA

Punta del Agua

Play

2

ISLA GRAC.

Punta del
Caleta del Mo

O C É A N O

Punta de las Carreras

3

Montaña

Punta del Pobre
Playa de la Cocina
Punta Marra

del Archip

4

A T L Á N T I C O

Pun

5

Chinijo

Pu

Punta Guerra

LAS BAJAS

Play
de Famar

El Rebolaje Machin

LA ISLETA Punta Prieta
Club
La Santa
La Costa
Caleta
de Caballo

Ermita
de San Juan
Bajamar

Playa de
San Juan

6

La Santa

Caldera Trasera

293

Sóo

La Caleta
de Famara

Casa del Molino

Urbanización
Famara

128

124

Urbanización
Vista Graciosa

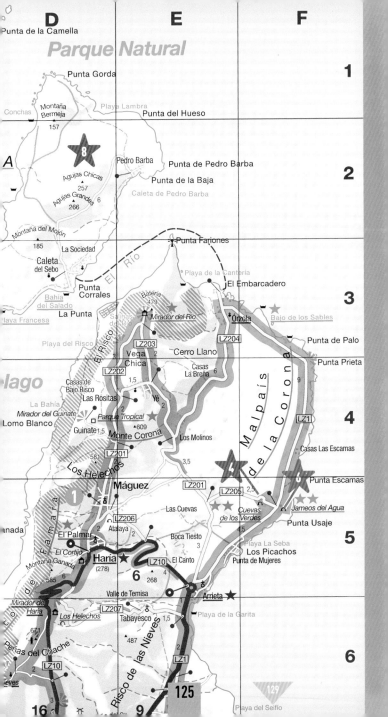

D

E

F

Punta de la Camella

Parque Natural

1

Punta Gorda

Conchas

Montaña
Bermeja
157

Playa Lambra

Punta del Hueso

A

⭐ **8**

Pedro Barba

Punta de Pedro Barba

Aguijas Chicas
257

Punta de la Baja

2

Aguijas Grandes
266

6

Caleta de Pedro Barba

Montaña del Mojón

185

Punta Fariones

La Sociedad

El Río

Playa de la Cantería

Caleta
del Sebo

El Embarcadero

3

Punta
Corrales

Bahía
del Salado

Batería
479

Órzola

Bajo de los Sables ⭐

La Punta

Salinas del Río

Mirador del Río ⭐

LZ204

Punta de Palo

laya Francesa

Playa del Risco

LZ203

Cerro Llano

Punta Prieta

lago

Vega
Chica

2

Casas
La Breña

6

M
a
l
p
a
í
s

9

LZ202

1,5

d
e

l
a

4

Casas de
Bajo Risco

2

Yé

Ye

C
o
r
o
n
a

LZ1

La Bahía

Mirador del Guinate

□ *Parque Tropical* ⭐

▲609

Lomo Blanco

Guinate 1,5

Monte Corona

Los Molinos

Casas Las Escamas

581 ▲

LZ201

3,5

⭐ ⭐

Los Helechos

Punta Escamas ⭐

L
a

Máguez

LZ201

LZ205 2,5

⭐ ⭐ ⭐

Jameos del Agua

G
a
n
a
d
a

Las Cuevas

⭐ ⭐
*Cuevas
de los Verdes*

Punta Usaje

5

anada

LZ206

2

Boca Tiesto

1,5

Playa La Seba

El Palmar ⭐

Atalaya

2

3

Los Picachos

El Cortijo

Haria ⭐

LZ10

El Canto

Punta de Mujeres

Montaña Ganada

(278)

4

585

6

268

*Mirador de
Haría* □

Valle de Temisa

Arrieta ⭐

R
i
s
c
o

d
e

LZ207

Playa de la Garita

Los Helechos

Tabayesco 1,5

671 ▲

487 ▲

Peñas del Chache

LZ10

R
i
s
c
o

d
e

l
a
s

N
i
e
v
e
s

LZ1

6

ieves

2

3

125

129

Playa del Seifío

16

9

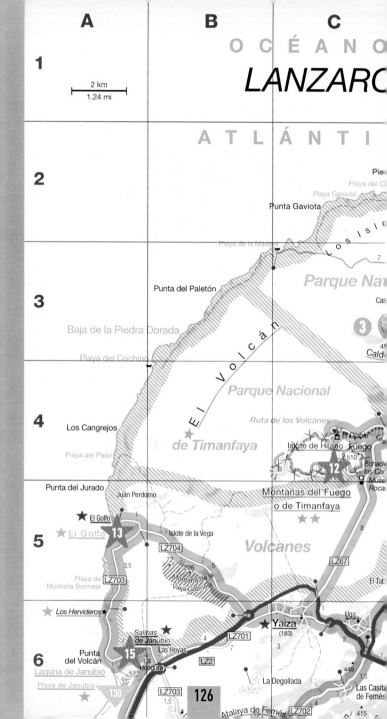

	A	B	C
1			
2			
3			
4			
5			
6			

O C É A N O

LANZARO

2 km
1.24 mi

A T L Á N T I

Pie

Playa del C

Playa Gaviota

Punta Gaviota

Los Islo

7

Parque Na

Playa de la Madera

Cas

Punta del Paletón

Punta del Paletón

Baja de la Piedra Dorada

El Volcán

4°

Cald

Playa del Cochino

Parque Nacional

Los Cangrejos

Ruta de los Volcanes

El Diablo

Playa del Paso

de Timanfaya

Islote de Hilario

Fuego

510

Echade

los Car

Muse

Punta del Jurado

Juan Perdomo

Roca

Montañas del Fuego

o de Timanfaya

★ El Golfo

El Golfo **13**

Islote de la Vega

Volcanes

LZ704

LZ67

72

El Tat

3,5

226

5

LZ703

Montaña de la

Vieja Gabriela

Playa de

Montaña Bermeja

8

Los Hervideros ★

Yaiza

Uga

(183)

Salinas

de Janubio ★

LZ701

1

Punta

del Volcán **15**

Las Hoyas

4

LZ2

3

449

Laguna de Janubio

La

Hondura

LZ703

7

1,5

Playa de Janubio

★

130

La Degollada

Las Casita

de Femés

LZ703

126

1,5

415

Atalaya de Femés LZ702

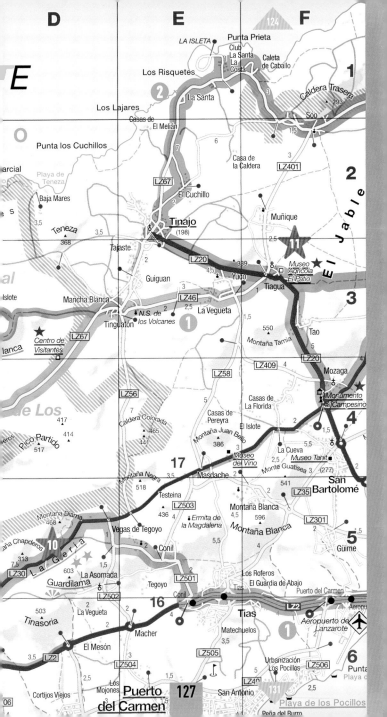

D   E   F

124

LA ISLETA   Punta Prieta

Club La Santa
La Santa
La Costa
Caleta de Caballo

Los Risquetes   **2**

La Santa

Caldera Trasera

Sóo
293

Los Lajares

Casas de El Melián

1,5

Punta los Cuchillos

Casa de la Caldera

LZ401

O

cial

Playa de Teneza

Baja Mares

7

6

3

Teneza
368

3,5

El Cuchillo

Muñique

2

2,5

2

El Jable

Tajaste

Tinajo
(198)

339

Yuco

Museo Agrícola El Patio

11

Guiguan

LZ20

4,5

Tiagua

Mancha Blanca

LZ46

2,5

La Vegueta

1

1,5

3

Tinguatón

N.S. de los Volcanes

3

2

Montaña Tamia

550

Tao

5

LZ67

Centro de Visitantes

lanca

Islote

1

de Los

417

LZ58

LZ409   4

LZ20

Mozaga

Monumento al Campesino

4

414

Pico Partido
517

LZ56

Caldera Colorada

7

465
441

Casas de La Florida

El Islote

1,5

ñeros

La Cueva

5,5

Casas de Pereyra

5

Montaña Juan Bello
386

Museo del Vino

2,5

Museo Tanit

San Bartolomé

Montaña Negra
518

17

3,5

Masdache

2

Monte Guatisea 3 (277)

541

2

Testeina

LZ503

436 4

Montaña Blanca
596

LZ35

Montaña Diama
468

Ermita de la Magdalena

4,5

Montaña Blanca

LZ301

5,5

ña Chapderos

10

313
7,5

603

Vegas de Tegoyo

2

Conil

2

Los Roferos
El Guardia de Abajo

Güime

5

1,5

1,5

La Asomada

LZ30

Guardilama

LZ502

Tegoyo

LZ501

2

Conil

Tias

Puerto del Carmen

LZ22

503

La Vegueta

2

16

2

4

Conil

1

Aeropuerto de Lanzarote

Tinasoria

Macher

Tias

Matechuelos

3,5

3,5 LZ2

El Mesón

3

LZ504

2,5

Los Mojones

1,5

LZ505

Urbanización Los Pocillos

5

LZ506

LZ4

Punta

Playa d

Cortijos Viejos

06

Puerto del Carmen

127

San Antonio

131

2,5

Playa de los Pocillos

Peña del Burro

La Gería

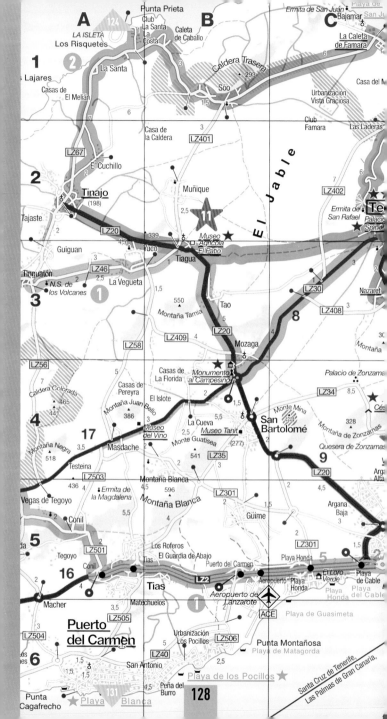

A **B** **C**

Punta Prieta
Ermita de San Juan
Playa de
Bajamar · San Ju

124

LA ISLETA
Los Risquetes
Club
La Santa
La Costa
Caleta
de Caballo
La Caleta
de Famara

1

2

La Santa
Caldera Trasera
293

Casas de
El Melián
Sóo
Casa del M
15
Urbanización
Vista Graciosa
6
7
Las Lajares

Casa de
la Caldera
3
Club
Famara
Las Laderas

LZ67
LZ401

El Cuchillo
2
E l   J a b l e
7
6

2

Tinajo
(198)
Muñique
LZ402

Tajaste
2.5
★**11**
Ermita de
San Rafael
Palacio
Spinol
Te

2
LZ20
339
Museo
Agrícola
El Patio ★

Guiguan
4.5
Yuco
Tiagua

Tinguatón
3
LZ46
2.5
La Vegueta
1.5
LZ30
Nazaret

3

N.S. de
los Volcanes
1
Tao
LZ408

550
Montaña Tamia
5
LZ20
8
30
Montaña

LZ58
LZ409
4
Mozaga
4

LZ56

7
Caldera Colorada
465
441
Casas de
La Florida
★
Monumento
al Campesino
2
1.5
Palacio de Zonzama
LZ34
8.5
Cés ★

4

Casas de
Pereyra
El Islote
La Cueva
5.5
San
Bartolomé
Monte Mina
Montaña de Zonzamas
328

Montaña Juan Bello
386
3
Museo
del Vino
2.5
Museo Tanit
(277)
Montaña de Zonzamas
Quesera de Zonzamas

17
Masdache
Monte Guatisea

Montaña Negra
3.5
541
LZ35

518
Testeina
LZ20
9

LZ503
Montaña Blanca
4.5
LZ301
Arg
Alta

436
4
Ermita de
la Magdalena
596
Argana
Baja
3

Vegas de Tegoyo
5.5
Montaña Blanca
Güime
2
4.5

Conil
2
LZ301
1.5

5
Tegoyo
LZ501
2
Playa Honda
5
Playa
de Cable
2

Conil
Los Roferos
El Guardia de Abajo
Puerto del Carmen
El Loro
Verde
1.5

16
4
Tías
LZ2
Aeropuerto
Playa
Honda
Playa
del Cable

Macher
Matechuelos
Aeropuerto de
Lanzarote
1
Playa
Honda
Playa de Guasimeta

3.5
LZ505

Puerto
del Carmen
Urbanización
Los Pocillos
LZ506
Punta Montañosa
Playa de Matagorda

LZ504
5
LZ40
2.5

6
1.5
San Antonio
Playa de los Pocillos ★

1.5
Peña del
Burro
128
Santa Cruz de Tenerife,
Las Palmas de Gran Canaria,

Punta
Cagafrecho
★ *Playa* *Blanca*
131

Playa de Famara

D

Risco de Famara

Playa de Famara

Los Helechos

Tabayesco

Playa de la Garita

E

F

671

125

de

Peñas del Chache

487

LZ1

2

Urbanización Famara

Ermita de las Nieves

LZ10

Peña de las Nieves

El Cangrejo

1.5

1

2

3

Mala

Playa del Seifio

Los Valles

16

Parque Eolico

Peña del Silvo
304

Los Ancabales

9

3.5

Museo

5

3

Charco del Palo

Urb. ANAC

Ermita

2.5

Risco

Jardín de Cactus

Guatiza

2

Ermita de San José

1.5

LZ406

Urbanización Los Cocoteros

se

3.5

Ermita de San Sebastián
El Mojón
(260)

1

323

3.5

452

2

1.5

Cast. de Santa Barbara

LZ404

2.5

Tinamala

Playa del Tío Joaquin

Guanapay

Teseguite

1

Omar

Urbanización Oasis de Nazaret

LZ1

7

4

Las Honduras

3

Las Mesetas

0

Urbanización Las Cabreras

3

3

235

Punta de Tierra Negra

3

Tahiche

321

Montaña Corona

ndación
anrique

Tahiche

1.5

6

2

3

El Rostro

2

Punta de la Corvina

4

LZ1

4

8

El Charco

Granados de Tahiche

2.5

Costa
Teguise

4.5

Playa de las Cucharas

Punta de Tope

LZ14

Playa Bastián

Las Caletas

Punta de Lomo Gordo

LZ3

1.5

4

1.5

Punta Grande

Playa de la Arena

Huelva, Cádiz

4

1.5

3

1

Cast. de San José

ISLA DE GRUCES

ISLA DEL FRANCES
Cast. de San Gabriel

0.5

ISLOTE
ERMINA

Punta de la Lagarta

Arrecife

2

5

uerto del Rosario
(Fuerteventura)

2 km

1.24 mi

6

129

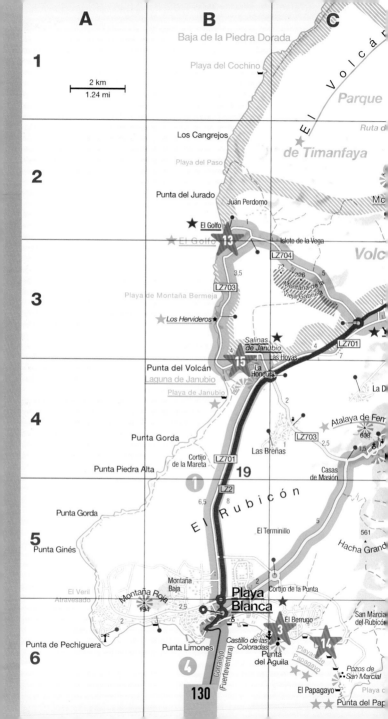

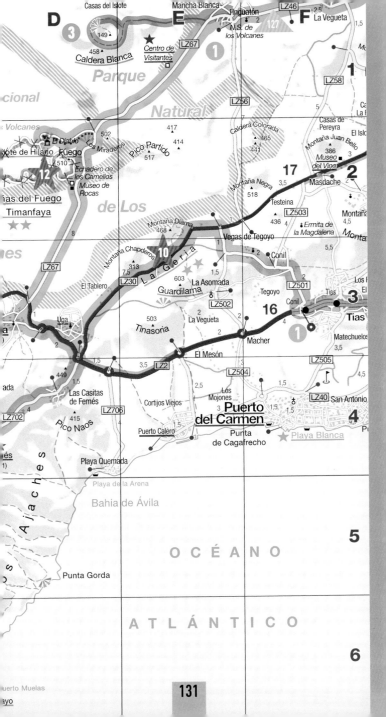

D 3

Casas del Islote

149 ▲

458 ▲ Caldera Blanca

Centro de Visitantes

Parque

cional

Natural

E

Mancha Blanca

Tinguatón

M.S. de los Volcanes

LZ67

1

LZ46

127

F 2.5 La Vegueta

1.5

1

LZ58

Mo

LZ56

5

Ca La

Volcanes

502

ote de Hilario

El Diablo

Fuego

510

Echadero de los Camellos

Museo de Rocas

Los Miraderos

Pico Partido

517

417

414 ▲

Caldera Colorada

465

441

Casas de Pereyra

El Islo

386

Museo del Vino

Montaña Juan Bello

3

2

12

as del Fuego

Timanfaya

★★

de Los

Montaña Diama

468 ▲

Montaña Negra

518

Testeina

436 4

Ermita de la Magdalena

3,5

Masdache

17

LZ503

Montaña

4,5

Monta

es

8

Montaña Chapderos

313

7,5

LZ30

El Tablero

1

Vegas de Tegoyo

10

La Gleria

★★

603

1,5

2

Conil

5,5

LZ67

La Asomada

Guardilama

LZ502

503

Tinasoria

La Vegueta

2

Tegoyo

LZ501

2

Los F

El

Tías

Conil

16

2

4

3

Tías

Matechuelos

3,5

a

1

Uga

449

1,5

1,5

2

3,5

LZ2

Macher

El Mesón

3

LZ504

LZ505

4,5

ada

Las Casitas de Femés

LZ706

Cortijos Viejos

2,5

Los Mojones

1,5

LZ40

San Antonio

LZ702

415

Pico Naos

Puerto Calero

Puerto del Carmen

Punta de Cagafrecho

1,5

1,5

Playa Blanca

4

P

és

s Ajaches

Playa Quemada

Playa de la Arena

Bahía de Ávila

Punta Gorda

O C É A N O

5

A T L Á N T I C O

6

uerto Muelas

ayo

KEY TO ROAD ATLAS

German	Symbol	English
Autobahn · Gebührenpflichtige Anschlussstelle · Gebührenstelle · Anschlussstelle mit Nummer · Rasthaus mit Übernachtung · Raststätte · Kleinraststätte · Tankstelle · Parkplatz mit und ohne WC	Trento	Motorway · Toll junction · Toll station · Junction with number · Motel · Restaurant · Snackbar · Filling-station · Parking place with and without WC
Autobahn in Bau und geplant mit Datum der voraussichtlichen Verkehrsübergabe	Datum / Date	Motorway under construction and projected with expected date of opening
Zweibahnstraße (4-spurig)		Dual carriageway (4 lanes)
Fernverkehrsstraße · Straßennummern	14 / E45	Trunk road · Road numbers
Wichtige Hauptstraße		Important main road
Hauptstraße · Tunnel · Brücke		Main road · Tunnel · Bridge
Nebenstraßen		Minor roads
Fahrweg · Fußweg		Track · Footpath
Wanderweg (Auswahl)		Tourist footpath (selection)
Eisenbahn mit Fernverkehr		Main line railway
Zahnradbahn, Standseilbahn		Rack-railway, funicular
Kabinenschwebebahn · Sessellift		Aerial cableway · Chair-lift
Autofähre · Personenfähre		Car ferry · Passenger ferry
Schifffahrtslinie		Shipping route
Naturschutzgebiet · Sperrgebiet		Nature reserve · Prohibited area
Nationalpark · Naturpark · Wald		National park · natural park · Forest
Straße für Kfz. gesperrt	X X X X X	Road closed to motor vehicles
Straße mit Gebühr		Toll road
Straße mit Wintersperre	XII-III	Road closed in winter
Straße für Wohnanhänger gesperrt bzw. nicht empfehlenswert		Road closed or not recommended for caravans
Touristenstraße · Pass	Weinstraße · 1510	Tourist route · Pass
Schöner Ausblick · Rundblick · Landschaftlich bes. schöne Strecke		Scenic view · Panoramic view · Route with beautiful scenery
Heilbad · Schwimmbad		Spa · Swimming pool
Jugendherberge · Campingplatz		Youth hostel · Camping site
Golfplatz · Sprungschanze		Golf-course · Ski jump
Kirche im Ort, freistehend · Kapelle		Church · Chapel
Kloster · Klosterruine		Monastery · Monastery ruin
Synagoge · Moschee		Synagogue · Mosque
Schloss, Burg · Schloss-, Burgruine		Palace, castle · Ruin
Turm · Funk-, Fernsehturm		Tower · Radio-, TV-tower
Leuchtturm · Kraftwerk		Lighthouse · Power station
Wasserfall · Schleuse		Waterfall · Lock
Bauwerk · Marktplatz, Areal		Important building · Market place, area
Ausgrabungs- u. Ruinenstätte · Bergwerk		Arch. excavation, ruins · Mine
Dolmen · Menhir · Nuraghen		Dolmen · Menhir · Nuraghe
Hünen-, Hügelgrab · Soldatenfriedhof		Cairn · Military cemetery
Hotel, Gasthaus, Berghütte · Höhle		Hotel, inn, refuge · Cave

Kultur — **Culture**

German	Symbol	English
Malerisches Ortsbild · Ortshöhe	WIEN (171)	Picturesque town · Elevation
Eine Reise wert	★★ MILANO	Worth a journey
Lohnt einen Umweg	★ TEMPLIN	Worth a detour
Sehenswert	Andermatt	Worth seeing

Landschaft — **Landscape**

German	Symbol	English
Eine Reise wert	★★ Las Cañadas	Worth a journey
Lohnt einen Umweg	★ Texel	Worth a detour
Sehenswert	Dikti	Worth seeing

German	Symbol	English
MARCO POLO Erlebnistour 1		**MARCO POLO Discovery Tour 1**
MARCO POLO Erlebnistouren		**MARCO POLO Discovery Tours**
MARCO POLO Highlight	★	**MARCO POLO Highlight**

MARCO POLO TRAVEL GUIDES

The travel guides with
Insider Tips

INDEX

This index lists all places and destinations as well as out-of-town beaches and sights featured in this guide. Numbers in bold indicate a main entry

CREDITS

WRITE TO US

e-mail: info@marcopologuides.co.uk

Did you have a great holiday?
Is there something on your mind?
Whatever it is, let us know!
Whether you want to praise, alert us
to errors or give us a personal tip –
MARCO POLO would be pleased to
hear from you.
We do everything we can to provide
the very latest information for your trip.

Nevertheless, despite all of our authors'
thorough research, errors can creep
in. MARCO POLO does not accept any
liability for this. Please contact us by
e-mail or post.

MARCO POLO Travel Publishing Ltd
Pinewood, Chineham Business Park
Crockford Lane, Chineham
Basingstoke, Hampshire RG24 8AL
United Kingdom

PICTURE CREDITS

Cover photo: Yaiza (Getty Images/Look: S. Lubenow)
Photos: DuMont Bildarchiv: Widmann (9); R. Freyer (30/31); I. Gawin (19 bottom); Getty Images: J. S. Callahan (2); Getty Images/AFP: D. Martin (22, 108/109); Getty Images/Look: S. Lubenow (1); huber-images: S. Lubenow (84, 96), Ripani (12/13), R. Schmid (17, 34, 78); laif: M. Amme (4 bottom, 26/27, 38/39, 70, 104/105), H. Eid (29), P. Frilet (75), G. Haenel (42, 111, 117), G. Knechtel (28 left, 110 bottom), J. Modrow (81), T. & B. Morandi (20/21), Tophoven (82); laif/hemis.fr: L. Montico (46, 102); laif/hemis.fr/Le Tourneur d'Ison (7); laif/robertharding: J. Miller (62); Look: F. M. Frei (25), S. Lubenow (64), J. Richter (90); Look/age fotostock (92); Look/Blend Images (67); mauritius images: K.-G. Dumrath (8), M. Lange (32/33, 69), R. Mirau (18 o.), O. Stadler (flap left, 54), M. Zurek (76/77); mauritius images/ableimages: D. Harrigan (18 bottom); mauritius images/age (50/51); mauritius images/age fotostock: N. Tondini (28 right); mauritius images/Alamy (3, 14/15, 106), A. Hartley (37), D. Kilpatrick (31), U. Kraft (58/59), J. Kruse (40/41); mauritius images/a-plus image bank/Alamy (30); mauritius images/CuboImages (58); mauritius images/graham bell travel/Alamy (flap right); mauritius images/ib/White Star: M. Gumm (53); mauritius images/imagebroker: U. Kraft (45), M. Lange (122/123), H. Laub (5, 100/101), M. Rucker (88/89), Siepmann (11), O. Stadler (72/73); mauritius images/imagebroker/White Star: M. Gumm (10); mauritius images/Prisma: R. van der Meer (6, 57, 110 top); mauritius images/Robert Harding (87); mauritius images/Wavebreakmedia (19 top); mauritius images/Westend61: M. Moxter (49); mauritius images/Wild Places Photography/Alamy: C. Howes (18 centre); D. Renckhoff (108); White Star: Schiefer (4 top, 60/61); T. P. Widmann (71)

3rd Edition – fully revised and updated 2018

Worldwide Distribution: Marco Polo Travel Publishing Ltd, Pinewood, Chineham Business Park, Crockford Lane, Basingstoke, Hampshire RG24 8AL, United Kingdom. Email: sales@marcopolouk.com
© MAIRDUMONT GmbH & Co. KG, Ostfildern
Chief editor: Marion Zorn
Author: Sven Weniger; co-author: Izabella Gawin; editor: Jens Bey, Karin Liebe
Programme supervision: Lucas Forst-Gill, Susanne Heimburger, Johanna Jiranek, Nikolai Michaelis, Kristin Wittemann, Tim Wohlbold
Picture editor: Gabriele Forst, Stefanie Wiese; What's hot: wunder media, Munich; Izabella Gawin
Cartography road atlas and pull-out map: © MAIRDUMONT, Ostfildern
Design cover, p. 1, cover pull-out map: Karl Anders – Büro für Visual Stories, Hamburg; interior design: milchhof:atelier, Berlin; p. 2/ 3, Discovery Tours: Susan Chaaban Dipl.-Des. (FH)
Translated from German by Paul Fletcher, Jennifer Walcoff Neuheiser, Andrea Scheuer
Prepress: writehouse, Cologne
Phrase book in cooperation with Ernst Klett Sprachen GmbH, Stuttgart, Editorial by Pons Wörterbücher

MIX
Paper from
responsible sources
FSC® C124385
www.fsc.org

DOS & DON'TS ✍

A few things to bear in mind on Lanzarote

DON'T TAKE ALONG EXOTIC PLANTS

Canary Island spurge, *arborescent launaea,* and the Canary Island daisy: don't give in to temptation and dig out the island's plants, roots and all, to take with you to your balcony at home. Canary Island plants are protected and their export is prohibited in most cases (customs!). However, that doesn't mean you have to do completely without: bags of seeds are available for purchase at any nursery *(jardinería)* – which is much easier to transport anyway!

DON'T JUMP INTO RED-FLAGGED WATERS

Year after year, dozens of people drown on the shores of the Canary Islands. The reason is often imprudence: they underestimate the strength of surf and currents, while overestimating their own strength. Always pay attention to the flags on the beaches and heed their warnings: when the red flag is raised, you should not enter the water, the yellow flag tells you to take care, and the green flag reassures you that it is safe to go throw yourself into the waves – but don't swim too far out. By the way: anyone who ignores a red flag and then needs rescuing has to pay for these services themselves!

DON'T WEAR LIGHT CLOTHING INTO THE MOUNTAINS

Flip-flops for a day in the mountains? The starting point for a tour of Lanzarote's highest mountain, the Peñas del Chache, is usually the sunny coast and so tourists head off in light, airy clothing only to be unpleasantly surprised by the clouds and cool winds when they reach the top. As a rule-of-thumb: temperatures drop by 1°C/34°F with every 100 metres gained in altitude. Therefore, if the temperatures at the coast are a balmy 23°C/74°F, the temperatures on the 700 m / 2297 ft high summit can be a quite cool 16°C/61°F when you get out of your car. And when you then factor in the generally strong winds on the summit, the real feel temperature will be even lower. So be sure to take a warm jacket with you on any trip into the mountains.

DON'T THROW TOILET PAPER INTO THE TOILET

You will surely find it odd, but many restrooms request that you refrain from "dropping any paper into the toilet". This may seem unhygienic to you, but unfortunately, the pipes in many older Canary Island houses are so narrow that they easily become clogged. It therefore makes sense to throw the used toilet paper into the bin provided – and the same goes for tissues, sanitary towels and tampons.

DON'T PAY TOO MUCH FOR THE INTERNET IN HOTELS

Many hotels offer their guests internet access or WiFi. But the cost of surfing the worldwide web quickly mounts up. Complain at hotel reception. Nowadays this service should be free everywhere.